SIE Exam

Practice Question Workbook

Coventry House Publishing

CONTENTS

PRACTICE EXAM 1

QUESTIONS

1. Which of the following corporate voting procedures entitles a shareholder to one vote per share, and votes must be divided evenly among the candidates being voted on?

   A. Accumulated voting
   B. Cumulative voting
   C. Non-regulatory voting
   D. Statutory voting

2. Which of the following refers to the trading of exchange-listed securities in the over-the-counter market? These trades allow institutional investors to trade blocks of securities directly, rather than through an exchange, providing liquidity and anonymity to buyers.

   A. First market
   B. Second market
   C. Third market
   D. Fourth market

3. An investor sells a naked call on Omikron for a $250 premium. Which of the following is true regarding the investor's position?

   A. The investor is expecting Omikron stock to increase in value.
   B. The investor's potential loss is unlimited.
   C. The investor's potential loss is limited to $250.
   D. The investor's outlook for Omikron stock is bullish.

4. Which of the following acts created the SEC and empowered it with broad authority over all aspects of the securities industry?

   A. Securities Act of 1933
   B. Securities Exchange Act of 1934
   C. Investment Advisers Act of 1940
   D. Investment Company Act of 1940

5. Which of the following is a free tool provided by FINRA that is intended to help consumers research the professional backgrounds of brokers and brokerage firms, as well as investment adviser firms and advisers?

   A. BrokerCheck
   B. FirmCheck
   C. InvestorCheck
   D. None of the above are correct.

6. The Federal Reserve Board performs which of the following actions?

    A. It sets monetary policy, but does not set tax policy.
    B. It sets tax policy, but does not set monetary policy.
    C. It sets monetary policy and tax policy.
    D. None of the above are correct.

7. Which of the following is an offering of shares to existing stockholders on a pro-rata basis?

    A. Private placement
    B. Public offering
    C. Rights offering
    D. Tender offering

8. The difference between a bond's price and the conversion parity price is referred to as which of the following?

    A. Bond premium
    B. Conversion premium
    C. Discount price
    D. Option premium

9. An individual who meets which of the following criteria must register as an investment adviser?

    (1) The individual provides advice or analyses concerning securities.
    (2) The individual is in the business of providing investment advice.
    (3) The individual provides investment advice for compensation.
    (4) The individual is a CPA or attorney whose investment advice is only incidental to his or her other activities.

    A. (3) only
    B. (1), (2), and (3) only
    C. (1), (2), and (4) only
    D. (2), (3), and (4) only

10. Which of the following is a type of preferred stock that gives the investor the right to receive dividends equal to the normally specified rate, as well as an additional dividend based on a specific predetermined condition?

    A. Accumulating preferred stock
    B. Dividend preferred stock
    C. Non-participating preferred stock
    D. Participating preferred stock

11. Profit sharing plans have which of the following characteristics?

    A. They favor older employees.

    B. They can be invested entirely in company stock.

    C. They are a type of defined contribution pension plan.

    D. The minimum funding standard requires the employer to make an annual contribution.

12. All but which of the following are correct regarding the Central Registration Depository (CRD)?

    A. It was developed by NASAA and the NASD.

    B. It consolidated a multiple paper-based state licensing and regulatory process into a single, nationwide computer system.

    C. Its computerized database contains the licensing and disciplinary histories on more than 650,000 securities professionals and 5,200 securities firms.

    D. All of the above are correct.

13. Which of the following are responsible for maintaining fair and orderly markets for an assigned set of listed firms? They operate both manually and electronically to facilitate price discovery during market opens, closes, and during periods of trading imbalances and instability.

    A. Certified Exchange Specialists

    B. Designated Market Makers

    C. Registered Floor Brokers

    D. Supplemental Liquidity Providers

14. If real GDP declined the last 3 quarters, how many more consecutive quarters of decline would be needed to be classified as an economic depression?

    A. 1 quarter

    B. 2 quarters

    C. 3 quarters

    D. 4 quarters

15. Which of the following is the correct reason to purchase a particular investment for a client's portfolio?

    A. Growth stocks because they pay high dividends.

    B. FNMA securities because they are backed by the full faith and credit of the U.S. government.

    C. Global fund because it provides only international exposure.

    D. Blue chip common stocks because they provide a hedge against inflation.

16. Which of the following is an unconditional promise to pay a sum of money to a payee, either at a fixed or determinable future time, under specific terms?

    A. Bank draft
    B. IOU
    C. Promissory note
    D. None of the above are correct.

17. A trade surplus results from which of the following?

    A. A country having a current account deficit.
    B. A country exporting more than it imports.
    C. A country exporting less than it imports.
    D. None of the above are correct.

18. William, age 56, recently retired from Epsilon Inc., and would like to take a distribution from a retirement plan to pay for medical expenses. Which of the following plans would allow William to take a penalty free withdrawal?

    A. Single premium deferred annuity
    B. Traditional IRA
    C. Money purchase plan from his employer before Epsilon Inc.
    D. 401(k) from Epsilon Inc.

For questions 19 – 22, match the stage of the business cycle with the description that follows. Use only one answer per blank. Answers may be used more than once or not at all.

    A. Trough
    B. Expansion
    C. Contraction
    D. Peak

19. ___ Recession

20. ___ Utilization at its lowest level

21. ___ Recovery

22. ___ GDP at its highest point

23. All but which of the following are characteristics of a REIT?

    A. It is a publicly traded open-end investment company.
    B. A mortgage REIT is a specific type of REIT.
    C. A REIT can sell at a premium or discount to its NAV.
    D. All of the above are correct.

24. Which of the following can an investor sign which allows him or her to receive break-point discounts based upon a commitment to buy a specified number of mutual fund shares over a period of time, usually 13 months?

    A. Investment advisory contract
    B. Investment memorandum
    C. Letter of intent
    D. Prospectus

25. Which of the following is a type of exchange rate system in which a country ties its currency to a basket of other currencies or to another measure of value, such as gold?

    A. Adjustable exchange rate system
    B. Commodity exchange rate system
    C. Fixed exchange rate system
    D. Variable exchange rate system

26. Which of the following will result if money distributed from a 529 plan is not used to pay for qualifying education expenses?

    A. The gain is taxed at capital gains rates, and a 10% penalty is applied.
    B. The gain is taxed at capital gains rates, and a 20% penalty is applied.
    C. The gain is taxed as ordinary income, and a 10% penalty is applied.
    D. The gain is taxed as ordinary income, and a 20% penalty is applied.

27. An investor who believes that an economic recession is imminent should purchase which of the following type of stocks?

    A. Defensive stocks because they tend to underperform during economic downturns.
    B. Defensive stocks because they tend to outperform during economic downturns.
    C. Cyclical stocks because they tend to outperform during economic downturns.
    D. Cyclical stocks because they tend to underperform during economic downturns.

28. Which of the following is/are correct regarding dividends paid by growth stocks and value stocks?

    (1) Because they are growing and expanding, growth stocks typically do not pay large dividends.
    (2) Most of the earnings generated from value stocks are reinvested back into the company.

    A. (1) only
    B. (2) only
    C. Both (1) and (2) are correct.
    D. Neither (1) or (2) are correct.

29. Which of the following is a type of broker that acts as a liaison between an investor and a clearing corporation by helping to ensure that trades are settled appropriately and transactions are successfully completed?

    A. Carrying broker
    B. Clearing broker
    C. Executing broker
    D. Introducing broker

30. Which of the following forms must broker-dealers, investment advisers, or issuers of securities fill out in order to terminate the registration of an individual in the appropriate jurisdiction? It is also known as the Uniform Termination Notice for Securities Industry Registration.

    A. Form U4
    B. Form U5
    C. Form U6
    D. Form U7

31. Which of the following is an order to sell a stock at a price below the current market price?

    A. Sell discount order
    B. Sell limit order
    C. Sell market order
    D. Sell stop order

32. Which of the following was adopted to update short sale regulations and to address concerns regarding potentially abusive naked short selling?

    A. Regulation BTR
    B. Regulation HFT
    C. Regulation NMS
    D. Regulation SHO

33. Which of the following is a fraudulent investment operation where the operator provides fabricated reports and generates investment returns for older investors through revenue paid by new investors, rather than from legitimate business activities or profits of financial trading?

    A. Pump and dump scheme
    B. Ponzi scheme
    C. Matrix scheme
    D. Bucket shop scheme

34. Which of the following is a self-regulatory organization (SRO)?

    A. FINRA
    B. NYSE
    C. SIPC
    D. All of the above are correct.

35. Which of the following is the largest options exchange in the U.S., and focuses on options contracts for individual equities and indexes?

    A. AMEX
    B. CBOE
    C. NASDAQ
    D. NYSE

36. Which of the following is the formula to calculate an investment's real return?

    A. Real return = Nominal return − Inflation
    B. Real return = Nominal return + Inflation
    C. Real return = Nominal return ÷ Inflation
    D. Real return = Inflation ÷ Nominal return

37. A currency transaction report (CTR) is a report that U.S. financial institutions are required to file with which of the following?

    A. FinCEN
    B. FINRA
    C. NAIC
    D. NASD

38. Investment advisers that have custody of client assets or require prepayment of advisory fees _____ or more in advance, and in excess of _____ for each client, must file an audited balance sheet with the SEC as of the end of the investment adviser's fiscal year.

    A. 6 months, $500
    B. 6 months, $1,000
    C. 12 months, $500
    D. 12 months, $1,000

39. All but which of the following are among the three categories of firm communications that are defined and regulated by FINRA Rule 2210?

    A. Correspondence
    B. Institutional communication
    C. Marketing communication
    D. Retail communication

40. Which of the following refers to the right to demand the repayment of monies paid if there has been a bad delivery of a stock or security?

A. Reclamation
B. Redemption
C. Rescission
D. Restriction

41. Which of the following is an advertisement used by a registered investment company that advises readers to obtain a full prospectus? It is not permitted to include an application to invest, and it must contain specific caveats pursuant to SEC Rule 482.

A. Omitting prospectus
B. Preliminary prospectus
C. Shelf registration
D. Tombstone ad

42. Which of the following is a note issued in which the government borrows money to finance a project and then repays lenders with revenue generated by the same project?

A. BAN
B. RAN
C. TAN
D. TRAN

43. Which of the following is a type of public offering auction in which the price of the offering is set after taking in all bids to determine the highest price at which the total offering can be sold?

A. American auction
B. Canadian auction
C. Dutch auction
D. European auction

44. In addition to the federal securities laws, each state has its own set of securities laws, commonly referred to as _____, which are designed to protect investors against fraudulent sales practices and activities.

A. Blue ocean laws
B. Blue sky laws
C. Green field laws
D. Open sky laws

45. Which of the following passes capital gains, dividends, and interest earned on fund investments directly to shareholders so that it is taxed only at the personal level, and double taxation is avoided?

    A. Private placement
    B. Regulated investment company
    C. Unregulated investment company
    D. Wholly owned subsidiary

46. In any single life private annuity transaction, if the seller outlives his or her actuarial life expectancy, the purchaser will have paid _____ for the property. If the seller does not outlive his or her actuarial life expectancy, the _____ will have made a good financial deal.

    A. too much, purchaser
    B. too much, seller
    C. too little, purchaser
    D. too little, seller

47. How is the net asset value (NAV) of a mutual fund calculated?

    A. NAV = (Total value of investment + Liabilities) ÷ Shares outstanding
    B. NAV = (Total value of investment ÷ Shares outstanding) – Liabilities
    C. NAV = (Total value of investment – Liabilities) ÷ Shares outstanding
    D. NAV = Total value of investment ÷ Shares outstanding

48. The statement of cash flows is separated into all but which of the following categories?

    A. Cash flow from financing activities
    B. Cash flow from income activities
    C. Cash flow from investing activities
    D. Cash flow from operating activities

49. Common stock is referred to as _____ because the owner of the stock is also an owner of the corporation and may participate in its capital and income growth.

    A. cumulative stock
    B. debt
    C. equity
    D. preferred stock

50. Which of the following is considered a hybrid security?

    A. Common stock
    B. Corporate bond
    C. Preferred stock
    D. REIT

51. Which of the following occurs when the supply of goods and services exceeds their demand?

    A. Deflation
    B. Inflation
    C. Stagflation
    D. Price stability

52. An IRA must be created and funded by _____ of the calendar year following the year in which the contribution applies.

    A. January 1
    B. April 15
    C. June 31
    D. December 31

53. Which of the following calculates the required amount of an employer's annual contribution to a defined benefit plan to ensure that current and future plan benefits are available to the participants?

    A. Administrator
    B. Actuary
    C. Broker
    D. Enrolled agent

54. The Bank Secrecy Act of 1970 requires financial institutions to assist U.S. government agencies in detecting and preventing money laundering by filing reports of cash transactions exceeding which of the following daily aggregate amounts?

    A. $5,000
    B. $10,000
    C. $50,000
    D. $100,000

55. A fixed income security is subject to which of the following risks?

    (1) Exchange rate risk
    (2) Purchasing power risk
    (3) Default risk
    (4) Liquidity risk
    (5) Reinvestment risk

    A. (1), (2), (3), and (4) only
    B. (1), (2), (4), and (5) only
    C. (2), (3), (4), and (5) only
    D. All of the above are correct.

For questions 56 – 60, match the investment with the description that follows. Use only one answer per blank. Each answer may be used only once.

   A. Money market fund
   B. Corporate bond
   C. Common stock
   D. Mutual fund
   E. Real estate

56. ___ Diversification smooths price volatility, historical above-inflation return, can pre-serve purchasing power in a portfolio.

57. ___ Liquid, easily converted to cash, low default risk, low real return.

58. ___ Fixed return, may lose value if not held until maturity, fixed interest payments.

59. ___ Not liquid, generally adequate inflation hedge.

60. ___ Used to generate income and growth, marketable, historical above-inflation re-turn, can preserve purchasing power in a portfolio.

61. Rob owns 200 shares of Epsilon stock, which recently announced that it will pay a 4% stock dividend. How many shares will Rob have after the dividend has been paid?

   A. 192 shares
   B. 200 shares
   C. 204 shares
   D. 208 shares

62. All but which of the following are correct regarding stock market benchmarks and in-dexes?

   A. The NASDAQ Composite is a value-weighted index.
   B. The Russell 2000 is a value-weighted index.
   C. The S&P 500 is a price-weighted index.
   D. The Wilshire 5000 is a value-weighted index.

63. Which of the following is an unconditional contract between a bond issuer and a bond-holder that specifies the terms of the bond?

   A. Debenture
   B. Indenture
   C. Prospectus
   D. Tombstone ad

64. Which of the following is/are correct regarding the capital structure of open-end mutual funds?

    (1) Open-end mutual funds issue new shares and redeem existing shares from shareholders.
    (2) The price an investor pays when buying shares of an open-end mutual fund is based on supply and demand.

    A. (1) only
    B. (2) only
    C. Both (1) and (2) are correct.
    D. Neither (1) or (2) are correct.

65. Which of the following refers to using property to secure payment of a loan, which includes mortgages, pledges, and putting up collateral, but the borrower retains possession?

    A. Hypothecate
    B. Pledge
    C. Remunerate
    D. None of the above are correct.

66. Which of the following is correct regarding Coverdell Education Savings Accounts (ESAs)?

    A. Private elementary school expenses are permitted to be paid from an ESA.
    B. The maximum annual contribution to an ESA is $5,000.
    C. Secondary school expenses are not permitted to be paid from an ESA.
    D. All of the above are correct.

67. The standard expiration period for a put or call option is _____. Long-term equity anticipation securities (LEAPS) have an expiration period _____.

    A. 6 months, longer than 1 year
    B. 6 months, between 6 months and 1 year
    C. 9 months, between 9 months and 1 year
    D. 9 months, longer than 1 year

68. A large interest rate change has the most significant effect on a _____ bond.

    A. low coupon
    B. short duration
    C. high coupon
    D. short maturity

69. All but which of the following are correct regarding the Federal Reserve?

    A. It derives its authority from Congress.
    B. It operates and oversees the U.S. payment system.
    C. It operates and oversees government spending.
    D. It supervises and regulates banks.

70. A mutual fund that invests in securities both inside and outside the U.S. is known as which of the following?

    A. Arbitrage fund
    B. Global fund
    C. International fund
    D. Long-short fund

71. Which of the following is correct regarding the taxation of TIPS?

    A. TIPS are taxed at the federal level only.
    B. TIPS are taxed at the state level only.
    C. TIPS are taxed at the state and federal level.
    D. TIPS are tax-free at both the state and federal level.

72. In 2017, the SEC adopted an amendment to the Settlement Cycle Rule under the Securities Exchange Act of 1934 that changed the standard settlement cycle for most broker-dealer transactions in which of the following ways?

    A. The standard settlement cycle was shortened from 3 business days after the trade (T+3) to 2 business days after the trade (T+2).
    B. The standard settlement cycle was shortened from 2 business days after the trade (T+2) to 1 business day after the trade (T+1).
    C. The standard settlement cycle was lengthened from 1 business day after the trade (T+1) to 2 business days after the trade (T+2).
    D. The standard settlement cycle was lengthened from 2 business days after the trade (T+2) to 3 business days after the trade (T+3).

73. Which of the following are permitted investments in an IRA?

    (1) Real estate
    (2) Money market funds
    (3) Common stock
    (4) Bond funds

    A. (3) and (4) only
    B. (1), (2), and (3) only
    C. (2), (3), and (4) only
    D. All of the above are correct.

74. Which of the following is/are correct regarding stock splits and reverse stock splits?

    (1) A 3-for-1 stock split will decrease a stock's market price per share.
    (2) A reverse stock split is intended to increase a stock's market price per share.

    A. (1) only
    B. (2) only
    C. Both (1) and (2) are correct.
    D. Neither (1) or (2) are correct.

75. Which of the following describes the relationship between total risk, systematic risk, and unsystematic risk?

    A. Total risk = Systematic risk – Unsystematic risk
    B. Total risk – Systematic risk = Unsystematic risk
    C. Total risk + Unsystematic risk = Systematic risk
    D. Unsystematic risk – Total risk = Systematic risk

ANSWER KEY

1. D
Statutory voting is a voting procedure in which each shareholder is entitled to one vote per share, and votes must be divided evenly among the candidates being voted on.

2. C
Third market refers to the trading of exchange-listed securities in the over-the-counter market. These trades allow institutional investors to trade blocks of securities directly, rather than through an exchange, providing liquidity and anonymity to buyers.

3. B
By selling a naked call, the investor is expecting Omikron's stock price to decrease. If the stock increases in value, the investor's potential loss is unlimited.

4. B
The Securities Exchange Act of 1934 created the SEC and empowered it with broad authority over all aspects of the securities industry.

5. A
BrokerCheck is a free tool provided by FINRA that is intended to help consumers research the professional backgrounds of brokers and brokerage firms, as well as investment adviser firms and advisers.

6. A
The Federal Reserve Board sets monetary policy, but does not set tax policy.

7. C
A rights offering is an offering of shares to existing stockholders on a pro-rata basis.

8. B
The difference between a bond's price and the conversion parity price is referred to as the conversion premium.

9. B
An individual who meets the following criteria must register as an investment adviser:
(1) The individual provides advice or analyses concerning securities.
(2) The individual is in the business of providing investment advice.
(3) The individual provides investment advice for compensation.

10. D
Participating preferred stock gives the investor the right to receive dividends equal to the normally specified rate, as well as an additional dividend based on a specific predetermined condition.

11. B
Profit sharing plans tend to favor younger employees, and they are not limited in their investment of company stock. Profit sharing plans are a type of defined contribution plan other than a pension plan. Their contributions must be substantial and recurring, but are not required annually.

12. D

The Central Registration Depository (CRD) was developed by NASAA and the NASD, and it consolidated a multiple paper-based state licensing and regulatory process into a single, nationwide computer system. Its computerized database contains the licensing and disciplinary histories on more than 650,000 securities professionals and 5,200 securities firms.

13. B

Designated Market Makers are responsible for maintaining fair and orderly markets for an assigned set of listed firms. They operate both manually and electronically to facilitate price discovery during market opens, closes, and during periods of trading imbalances and instability.

14. C

6 quarters – 3 quarters = 3 quarters

An economic depression is defined as a decline in real GDP for 6 or more consecutive quarters.

15. D

Blue chip common stocks provide a hedge against inflation. Growth stocks typically reinvest their earnings back into the company rather than pay dividends to shareholders. GNMA securities, not FNMA, are backed by the U.S. government. Global funds invest in both U.S. and international companies.

16. C

A promissory note is an unconditional promise to pay a sum of money to a payee, either at a fixed or determinable future time, under specific terms. An IOU differs from a promissory note in that an IOU does not specify repayment terms such as the time of repayment. A bank draft is a type of check in which the payment is guaranteed to be available by the issuing bank.

17. B

A trade surplus results from a country exporting more than it imports.

18. D

Withdrawals from a 401(k) after separating from service are penalty free if the separation occurs at age 55 or older. The other options would result in an early withdrawal penalty.

19. C

The contraction stage of the business cycle is characterized by recession.

20. A

At the trough of the business cycle, utilization will be at its lowest level.

21. B

The expansion stage of the business cycle is characterized by recovery.

22. D

At the peak of the business cycle, GDP will be at its highest point.

23. A
REITs are publicly traded closed-end investment companies that can sell at a premium or discount to its NAV. A mortgage REIT is a specific type of REIT.

24. C
An investor can sign a letter of intent (LOI) which allows him or her to receive breakpoint discounts based upon a commitment to buy a specified number of mutual fund shares over a period of time, usually 13 months.

25. C
In a fixed exchange rate system, a country ties its currency to a basket of other currencies or to another measure of value, such as gold.

26. C
If money distributed from a 529 plan is not used to pay for qualifying education expenses, the gain is taxed as ordinary income and a 10% penalty is applied.

27. B
An investor who believes that an economic recession is imminent should purchase defensive stocks because they tend to outperform during economic downturns.

28. A
Because they are growing and expanding, growth stocks typically do not pay large dividends. Most of the earnings generated from growth stocks are reinvested back into the company.

29. B
A clearing broker acts as a liaison between an investor and a clearing corporation by helping to ensure that trades are settled appropriately and transactions are successfully completed.

30. B
Broker-dealers, investment advisers, and issuers of securities must fill out form U5 in order to terminate the registration of an individual in the appropriate jurisdiction. It is also known as the Uniform Termination Notice for Securities Industry Registration.

31. D
A sell stop order is an order to sell a stock at a price below the current market price.

32. D
Regulation SHO was adopted to update short sale regulations and to address concerns regarding potentially abusive naked short selling.

33. B
A Ponzi scheme is a fraudulent investment operation where the operator provides fabricated reports and generates returns for older investors through revenue paid by new investors, rather than from legitimate business activities or profits of financial trading.

34. D
FINRA, NYSE, and SIPC are self-regulatory organizations (SROs).

35. B
The CBOE (Chicago Board Options Exchange) is the largest options exchange in the U.S. and focuses on options contracts for individual equities and indexes.

36. A
Real return = Nominal return – Inflation

37. A
A currency transaction report (CTR) is a report that U.S. financial institutions are required to file with FinCEN (Financial Crimes Enforcement Network).

38. A
Investment advisers that have custody of client assets or require prepayment of advisory fees 6 months or more in advance, and in excess of $500 for each client, must file an audited balance sheet with the SEC as of the end of the investment adviser's fiscal year.

39. C
The three categories of firm communications that are defined and regulated by FINRA Rule 2210 are correspondence, institutional communication, and retail communication.

40. A
Reclamation refers to the right to demand the repayment of monies paid if there has been a bad delivery of a stock or security.

41. A
An omitting prospectus is an advertisement used by a registered investment company that advises readers to obtain a full prospectus. It is not permitted to include an application to invest, and it must contain specific caveats pursuant to SEC Rule 482.

42. B
A RAN (revenue anticipation note) is a note issued in which the government borrows money to finance a project and then repays lenders with revenue generated by the same project.

43. C
A Dutch auction is a type of public offering auction in which the price of the offering is set after taking in all bids to determine the highest price at which the total offering can be sold.

44. B
In addition to the federal securities laws, each state has its own set of securities laws, commonly referred to as blue sky laws, which are designed to protect investors against fraudulent sales practices and activities.

45. B
A regulated investment company passes capital gains, dividends, and interest earned on fund investments directly to shareholders so that it is taxed only at the personal level, and double taxation is avoided.

46. A

In any single life private annuity transaction, if the seller outlives his or her actuarial life expectancy, the purchaser will have paid too much for the property. If the seller does not outlive his or her actuarial life expectancy, the purchaser will have made a good financial deal.

47. C

NAV = (Total value of investment – Liabilities) ÷ Shares outstanding

48. B

The statement of cash flows is separated into the following three categories: cash flow from financing activities, cash flow from investing activities, and cash flow from operating activities.

49. C

Common stock is referred to as equity because the owner of the stock is also an owner of the corporation and may participate in its capital and income growth.

50. C

Preferred stock is considered a hybrid security because it has characteristics of both common stock and fixed-income investments.

51. A

Deflation occurs when the supply of goods and services exceeds their demand.

52. B

An IRA must be created and funded by April 15 of the calendar year following the year in which the contribution applies.

53. B

An actuary calculates the required amount of an employer's annual contribution to a defined benefit plan to ensure that current and future plan benefits are available to the participants.

54. B

The Bank Secrecy Act of 1970 requires financial institutions to assist U.S. government agencies in detecting and preventing money laundering by filing reports of cash transactions exceeding $10,000 (daily aggregate amount).

55. D

A fixed income security may be subject to all of the risks listed. This includes systematic risks that are always present (exchange rate risk, purchasing power risk, reinvestment risk), as well as non-systematic risks, such as default risk and liquidity risk.

56. D

Mutual fund: Diversification smooths price volatility, historical above-inflation return, can preserve purchasing power in a portfolio.

57. A

Money market fund: Liquid, easily converted to cash, low default risk, low real return.

58. B
Corporate bond: Fixed return, may lose value if not held until maturity, fixed interest payments.

59. E
Real estate: Not liquid, generally adequate inflation hedge.

60. C
Common stock: Used to generate income and growth, marketable, historical above-inflation return, can preserve purchasing power in a portfolio.

61. D
200 shares + (200 shares × 0.04) = 208 shares

62. C
The NASDAQ Composite, Russell 2000, S&P 500, and Wilshire 5000 are value-weighted indexes.

63. B
An indenture is an unconditional contract between a bond issuer and a bondholder that specifies the terms of the bond.

64. A
Open-end mutual funds issue new shares and redeem existing shares from shareholders. The price an investor pays when buying shares of an open-end mutual fund is based on the fund's net asset value (NAV).

65. A
Hypothecate refers to using property to secure payment of a loan, which includes mortgages, pledges, and putting up collateral, but the borrower retains possession.

66. A
Money in a Coverdell Education Savings Account (ESA) may be used to pay private elementary and/or secondary school expenses. The maximum contribution to an ESA is $2,000 per beneficiary per year.

67. D
The standard expiration period for a put or call option is 9 months. Long-term equity anticipation securities (LEAPS) have an expiration period longer than 1 year.

68. A
A large interest rate change has the most significant effect on a low coupon bond.

69. C
The Federal Reserve supervises and regulates banks, and operates and oversees the U.S. payment system. It derives its authority from Congress.

70. B
A mutual fund that invests in securities both inside and outside the U.S. is known as a global fund.

71. A

TIPS (Treasury inflation-protected securities) are taxed at the federal level only.

72. A

As a result of the SEC adopting an amendment to the Settlement Cycle Rule under the Securities Exchange Act of 1934, the standard settlement cycle was shortened from 3 business days after the trade (T+3) to 2 business days after the trade (T+2).

73. D

IRAs may invest in all four types of investments, including real estate (REITs).

74. C

A 3-for-1 stock split will decrease a stock's market price per share. A reverse stock split is intended to increase a stock's market price per share.

75. B

Total risk = Systematic risk + Unsystematic risk.

This formula can be rewritten as: Total risk – Systematic risk = Unsystematic risk.

PRACTICE EXAM 2

QUESTIONS

1. How frequently will a mutual fund with a turnover ratio of 20% replace its total holdings?

   A. Every year
   B. Every 2 years
   C. Every 4 years
   D. Every 5 years

2. All but which of the following are considered securities under the Uniform Securities Act?

   A. Debentures
   B. Precious metals
   C. Variable annuities
   D. Variable life insurance

3. When a bond is selling at a premium to par, the yield to maturity (YTM) will always be _____ the bond's coupon rate. If a bond is selling at a discount to par, the YTM will always be _____ the bond's coupon rate.

   A. greater than, equal to
   B. greater than, less than
   C. less than, equal to
   D. less than, greater than

4. Which of the following elements of FINRA's Continuing Education Program focuses on compliance, ethical, and sales practice standards? Its content is derived from industry rules and regulations, and accepted standards and practices in the industry.

   A. Compliance Element
   B. Firm Element
   C. Regulatory Element
   D. Regulatory and Firm Elements

5. Which of the following imposed an obligation on the SEC to consider the impacts that any new regulation would have on competition, and empowered the SEC to establish a national market system and a system for nationwide clearing and settlement of securities transactions?

   A. Uniform Securities Act of 1956
   B. Securities Act Amendments of 1975
   C. Uniform Prudent Investors Act of 1994
   D. National Securities Market Improvement Act of 1996

6. Congress has provided which of the following entities with the power to supervise self-regulatory organizations (SROs) as a matter of public interest?

A. FINRA
B. MSRB
C. NASD
D. SEC

7. Which of the following is required by the IRS if a taxpayer uses the substantially equal periodic payment (SEPP) exception to the premature distribution penalty?

A. The taxpayer must show proof of economic hardship.
B. The taxpayer must show proof that payments will be used to pay for qualified medical or education expenses.
C. The taxpayer must show proof that appropriate taxes will be withheld.
D. None of the above are correct.

8. Which of the following is a person who, for compensation, makes recommendations regarding securities, manages client accounts, and determines which advice regarding securities should be given?

A. ADV
B. CRD
C. IAR
D. IARD

9. A long stock position is considered _____, and a short stock position is considered _____.

A. Bearish, bearish
B. Bearish, bullish
C. Bullish, bearish
D. Bullish, bullish

10. Pete, an elderly business owner, is interested in establishing a retirement plan that will provide the greatest retirement benefit to himself. Which of the following plans should Pete select?

A. Defined benefit plan
B. Defined contribution plan
C. Money purchase plan
D. 401(k) plan

11. The S&P index has _____ risk.

    A. non-systematic
    B. non-diversifiable
    C. diversifiable
    D. unsystematic

12. Which of the following mutual fund share classes will charge investors a back-end load?

    A. Class A shares
    B. Class B shares
    C. Class C shares
    D. Class D shares

13. Regulation A permits unregistered public offerings of up to _____ of securities in any 12-month period.

    A. $1 million
    B. $2 million
    C. $5 million
    D. $10 million

14. Which of the following is a requirement in which financial institutions need to verify the identity of individuals wishing to conduct financial transactions with them?

    A. Automated Client Account Transfer Service
    B. Customer Identification Program
    C. Trade Reporting and Compliance Engine
    D. None of the above are correct.

15. Which of the following forms of ownership allows an investor to own securities without a certificate?

    A. Book entry form
    B. Central entry form
    C. Custodian entry form
    D. Depository entry form

16. Which of the following has the mission of protecting investors, municipal entities, and the public interest by promoting a fair and efficient municipal market, regulating firms that engage in municipal securities and advisory activities, and promoting market transparency?

    A. AMBAC
    B. FNMA
    C. GNMA
    D. MSRB

For questions 17 – 19, match the real estate investment with the description that follows. Use only one answer per blank. Answers may be used more than once or not at all.

A. Equity REIT
B. Mortgage REIT
C. REMIC

17. ___ Invests in loans secured by real estate.

18. ___ Self-liquidating, flow-through entity that invests in real estate mortgages or mortgage-backed securities.

19. ___ Acquires ownership interests in commercial, industrial, and residential properties. Income is received from the rental of these properties.

20. According to FINRA Rule 3240, which of the following is correct regarding borrowing and lending arrangements between a Registered Investment Advisor and its customers?

A. The specific borrowing/lending arrangement must meet certain conditions, such as the customer cannot be an immediate family member.
B. Proper notification of the borrowing or lending arrangement must be given, but advanced approval is not required.
C. The member firm must have a written policy in place regarding borrowing and lending arrangements.
D. All of the above are correct.

21. Which of the following investments will provide tax-exempt interest if the proceeds are used to pay for qualifying education expenses?

(1) FNMA funds
(2) Series EE bonds
(3) Treasury bonds
(4) Treasury bills

A. (2) only
B. (1) and (2) only
C. (2), (3), and (4) only
D. All of the above are correct.

22. Which of the following type of bond is unregistered, with no record kept regarding the owner or transactions involving ownership?

A. Bearer bond
B. Brady bond
C. Fidelity bond
D. Surety bond

23. Which of the following is/are correct regarding liquidity and marketability?

    (1) Liquidity is the ability to sell or redeem an investment quickly and at a known price without incurring a significant loss of principal.
    (2) Marketability is the speed and ease with which an investment may be bought or sold.

    A. (1) only
    B. (2) only
    C. Both (1) and (2) are correct.
    D. Neither (1) or (2) are correct.

24. Which of the following are among the criteria to be an "accredited investor"?

    A. Net worth exceeding $500,000, either alone or together with a spouse, excluding the value of the person's primary residence.
    B. Net worth exceeding $500,000, either alone or together with a spouse, including the value of the person's primary residence.
    C. Net worth exceeding $1,000,000, either alone or together with a spouse, excluding the value of the person's primary residence.
    D. Net worth exceeding $1,000,000, either alone or together with a spouse, including the value of the person's primary residence.

25. All but which of the following are characteristics of American Depository Receipts (ADRs)?

    A. They are traded on secondary exchanges.
    B. They represent ownership interest in foreign securities denominated in U.S. dollars.
    C. They involve banks collecting money in U.S. dollars and then converting into foreign currency for ADR holders.
    D. They are issued by banks in foreign countries.

26. Which of the following accurately describes the difference between rights and warrants?

    (1) A warrant may be attached to new debt or preferred issues to make the issues more attractive to buyers.
    (2) Rights and warrants have different lifespans.
    (3) Warrants usually expire within a few weeks.
    (4) Rights may continue without expiring for up to several years.

    A. (1) only
    B. (1) and (2) only
    C. (2), (3), and (4) only
    D. All of the above are correct.

27. Which of the following is the governing body of FINRA, which oversees the administration of its affairs and the promotion of its welfare, objectives, and purposes?

    A. Board of Governors
    B. Board of Trustees
    C. Congress
    D. FINRA Chairman

28. Preferred stock that does not have to pay missed dividends is considered which of the following?

    A. Convertible
    B. Cumulative
    C. In-kind
    D. Noncumulative

29. Which of the following rules permits the public resale of restricted or control securities if a number of conditions are met, including how long the securities are held, the way in which they are sold, and the amount that can be sold at any one time?

    A. Securities Act Rule 144
    B. Securities Act Rule 405
    C. Securities Act Rule 433
    D. Securities Act Rule 506

30. Which of the following is/are correct regarding a flat yield curve?

    (1) It generally indicates an economic slowdown.
    (2) It occurs when there is little difference between short-term and long-term yields for debt instruments of the same credit quality.

    A. (1) only
    B. (2) only
    C. Both (1) and (2) are correct.
    D. Neither (1) or (2) are correct.

31. Which of the following SEC regulations requires firms to have policies and procedures addressing the protection of customer information and records? This regulation also requires firms to provide initial and annual privacy notices to customers describing information sharing policies.

    A. Regulation FD
    B. Regulation MA-W
    C. Regulation N-Q
    D. Regulation S-P

32. According to the Telephone Consumer Protection Act, solicitors are prohibited from calling residences before _____ and after _____ local time.

    A. 7 a.m., 10 p.m.
    B. 8 a.m., 9 p.m.
    C. 9 a.m., 5 p.m.
    D. 10 a.m., 8 p.m.

33. Which of the following describes the illegal practice of excessive buying and selling of securities in a customer's account without considering the customer's investment goals? Its primary goal is to generate commissions that benefit the broker.

    A. Capping
    B. Churning
    C. Front running
    D. Painting the tape

34. The two main types of mutual fund prospectuses are the _____ prospectus and the _____ prospectus.

    A. omitting, statutory
    B. preliminary, statutory
    C. preliminary, summary
    D. statutory, summary

35. Which of the following is the minimum denomination of Treasury notes that can be purchased by an investor?

    A. $50
    B. $100
    C. $1,000
    D. $10,000

36. Treasury STRIPS are always issued at a:

    A. premium to par.
    B. discount to par.
    C. price equal to par.
    D. price above or equal to par.

37. Which of the following is used to determine whether an instrument qualifies as an "investment contract" for the purposes of the Securities Act of 1933?

    A. The Howey test
    B. The Knight test
    C. The Lochner test
    D. The Ralston test

38. Which of the following securities are backed by the full faith and credit of the U.S. government?

    A. Federal Home Loan Mortgage Corporation debentures (Freddie Macs)
    B. Federal National Mortgage Association certificates (Fannie Maes)
    C. Government National Mortgage Association certificates (Ginnie Maes)
    D. Student Loan Marketing Association notes (Sallie Maes)

39. Which of the following refers to the high-speed electronic system that reports the latest price and volume data on sales of exchange-listed stocks?

    A. Consolidated tape
    B. Instinet
    C. EDGAR
    D. TRACE

40. All but which of the following are correct regarding a bond's call provision?

    A. It protects the issuer from declines in interest rates.
    B. It will cause the investor's required rate of return to be lower.
    C. It may be included in a bond agreement.
    D. It allows the debtor to pay off the debt after a specific period of time at a predetermined price.

41. In order to be eligible to make a traditional IRA contribution, an individual must be younger than age _____ by the end of the taxable year.

    A. 59 ½
    B. 65
    C. 70 ½
    D. 71

42. All but which of the following are correct regarding the Federal Open Market Committee (FOMC)?

    A. It consists of 12 members.
    B. It holds 8 regularly scheduled meetings per year.
    C. It reviews economic and financial conditions and determines the appropriate stance of monetary policy.
    D. All of the above are correct.

43. Which of the following lists the stages of money laundering in the correct order?

    A. Layering, integration, placement
    B. Layering, placement, integration
    C. Placement, integration, layering
    D. Placement, layering, integration

For questions 44 – 47, match the legislation with the description that follows. Use only one answer per blank. Answers may be used more than once or not at all.

    A. Securities Act of 1933
    B. Securities Exchange Act of 1934
    C. Investment Company Act of 1940
    D. Securities Investor Protection Act of 1970

44. ___ Regulates brokerage firms.

45. ___ Regulates mutual funds.

46. ___ Regulates new securities.

47. ___ Regulates existing securities.

48. If interest rates _____ following a bond issue, a sinking-fund provision will allow the issuing company to reduce the interest rate risk of its bonds as it replaces a portion of the existing debt with _____ bonds.

    A. decline, higher yielding
    B. decline, lower yielding
    C. rise, higher yielding
    D. rise, lower yielding

49. Which of the following refers to the inverse relationship between bond prices and an investor's required rate of return?

    A. Credit risk
    B. Interest rate risk
    C. Liquidity risk
    D. Reinvestment risk

50. Which of the following describes the process in which an underwriter intervenes in the secondary market by placing a bid for securities at or below the offering price? The goal is to protect the price from dropping if there is a lack of initial interest for a new issue.

    A. Stabilizing bid
    B. Standby underwriting
    C. Subscription underwriting
    D. Underwriting bid

51. Which of the following is an internal meeting between the officials of an organization that will be issuing securities and members of the syndicate that will be distributing them? The meeting is held after the registration of a new security with the SEC, but before the registration's effective date.

    A. Due diligence meeting
    B. Prospectus meeting
    C. Registration meeting
    D. Syndicate meeting

52. The annual report on _____ provides a comprehensive overview of a company's business and financial condition and includes audited financial statements.

    A. Form 6-K
    B. Form 8-K
    C. Form 10-K
    D. Form 10-Q

53. All but which of the following are types of municipal bonds?

    A. General obligation bond
    B. Preferred bond
    C. Private activity bond
    D. Revenue bond

54. Alex, age 70, has contributed $20,000 to a Roth IRA throughout his career. The account value is now $30,000. If Alex withdraws the entire amount, how much tax will he owe if he's in the 28% tax bracket?

    A. $0
    B. $1,500
    C. $4,500
    D. $8,400

55. During a recent recession, your client, Charles, purchased high-yield corporate bonds that now face minimal default risk. However, he's now concerned that the various corporations may decide to call their bonds. You tell Charles that corporations are likely to call their bonds when:

    A. interest rates are expected to drop.
    B. the bonds are selling at a significant premium.
    C. inflation is expected to rise.
    D. interest rates have declined.

56. Which of the following is an electronic filing system that facilitates investment adviser registration, exempt reporting adviser filing, regulatory review, and the public disclosure information of registered investment adviser firms and individuals?

    A. ADV
    B. CRD
    C. EDGAR
    D. IARD

57. Which of the following acts established the policies and procedures commonly referred to as a "Chinese wall"?

    A. Uniform Securities Act of 1956
    B. Bank Secrecy Act of 1970
    C. Insider Trading and Securities Fraud Enforcement Act of 1988
    D. Sarbanes-Oxley Act of 2002

58. Which of the following describes the relationship between a security's bid-ask spread and its liquidity?

    A. In general, the smaller a security's bid-ask spread, the better its liquidity.
    B. In general, the larger a security's bid-ask spread, the better its liquidity.
    C. The bid-ask spread effects a security's marketability, but not its liquidity.
    D. There is no relationship between a security's bid-ask spread and its liquidity.

59. Which of the following is a type of debt issued by a national government in a foreign currency in order to finance the issuing country's growth and development?

    A. Domestic debt
    B. Eurodebt
    C. Foreign debt
    D. Sovereign debt

60. The two broad categories of defined contribution plans are:

    A. defined benefit plans and pension plans.
    B. personal plans and employer plans.
    C. profit sharing plans and pension plans.
    D. qualified plans and profit sharing plans.

61. The Dow Jones Industrial Average is an index comprised of _____ industrial companies.

    A. 20
    B. 30
    C. 40
    D. 50

62. Which of the following determines the minimum margin requirement for investment accounts?

    A. Congress
    B. FDIC
    C. Federal Reserve
    D. SIPC

63. Regarding municipal bonds, which of the following is the small amount of money, usually less than 5% of an issue, that underwriters give to the issuer in exchange for the right to place part of the issue?

    A. Credit deposit
    B. Down payment
    C. Escrow deposit
    D. Good faith deposit

64. All but which of the following are correct regarding a UGMA/UTMA account?

    A. Unlike a 529 plan, funds do not need to be used to pay for education expenses.
    B. The custodian, typically the minor's parent, does not own the assets in the account.
    C. Similar to a 529 plan, funds in the account grow tax-deferred.
    D. Once the account is set up, it's considered to be an irrevocable gift.

65. A currency transaction report (CTR) must be filed by U.S. financial institutions for each deposit, withdrawal, exchange of currency, or other payment to the institution which involves a transaction in currency of more than:

    A. $5,000.
    B. $10,000.
    C. $25,000.
    D. $50,000.

For questions 66 – 69, match the hedging technique with the description that follows. Use only one answer per blank. Answers may be used more than once or not at all.

    A. Collar
    B. Spread
    C. Straddle
    D. Protective put

66. ___ Purchasing a call option and selling a call option on the same stock at the same time.

67. ___ Purchasing a put option and selling a call option on the same stock at the same time.

68. ___ Purchasing a put option while holding shares of the underlying stock from a previous purchase.

69. ___ Purchasing a call option and a put option on the same stock at the same time.

70. Which of the following is/are correct regarding a bond's coupon rate?

   (1) The smaller a bond's coupon, the greater its relative price fluctuation.
   (2) The smaller a bond's coupon, the greater its reinvestment risk.

   A. (1) only
   B. (2) only
   C. Both (1) and (2) are correct.
   D. Neither (1) or (2) are correct.

71. Which of the following describes the difference between a 401(k) plan and a 403(b) plan?

   A. A 401(k) plan is a qualified plan, and a 403(b) plan is not a qualified plan.
   B. A 403(b) plan is a qualified plan, and a 401(k) plan is not a qualified plan.
   C. A 401(k) plan allows loans, and a 403(b) plan does not allow loans.
   D. A 501(c)(3) organization may establish a 403(b) plan but cannot establish a 401(k) plan.

72. An investor purchased a share of Kappa stock for $184 and sold it for $173. If a $4.25 dividend was paid during the holding period, what was the total return?

   A. −4.67%
   B. −4.33%
   C. −4.02%
   D. −3.67%

73. A corporate insider is defined as a director or senior officer of a company, as well as any person or entity that beneficially owns more than _____ of a company's voting shares.

   A. 1%
   B. 2%
   C. 5%
   D. 10%

74. Which of the following is the typical limit on the term of a loan from a qualified retirement plan?

   A. 1 year
   B. 2 years
   C. 5 years
   D. 10 years

75. The Securities Acts Amendments of 1975 did which of the following?

    A. It gave authority to the Municipal Securities Rulemaking Board (MSRB).

    B. It required financial institutions to assist U.S. government agencies to detect and prevent money laundering.

    C. It provided fiduciary responsibilities for those who manage and control plan assets and gave participants the right to sue for benefits and breaches of fiduciary duty.

    D. It created the Public Company Accounting Oversight Board to oversee the activities of the auditing profession.

ANSWER KEY

1. D
$1 \div 0.20 = 5$
A mutual fund with a turnover ratio of 20% will replace its total holdings every 5 years.

2. B
Debentures, variable annuities, and variable life insurance are considered securities under the Uniform Securities Act. Precious metals are not considered securities.

3. D
When a bond is selling at a premium to par, the yield to maturity (YTM) will always be less than the bond's coupon rate. If a bond is selling at a discount to par, the YTM will always be greater than the bond's coupon rate.

4. C
The Regulatory Element of FINRA's Continuing Education Program focuses on compliance, ethical, and sales practice standards. Its content is derived from industry rules and regulations, and accepted standards and practices in the industry.

5. B
The Securities Act Amendments of 1975 imposed an obligation on the SEC to consider the impacts that any new regulation would have on competition, and empowered the SEC to establish a national market system and a system for nationwide clearing and settlement of securities transactions.

6. D
Congress has provided the SEC with the power to supervise self-regulatory organizations (SROs) as a matter of public interest.

7. D
For the substantially equal periodic payment (SEPP) exception to the premature distribution penalty, the IRS does not require a reason for taking withdrawals.

8. C
An IAR (investment adviser representative) is a person who, for compensation, makes recommendations regarding securities, manages client accounts, and determines which advice regarding securities should be given.

9. C
A long stock position is considered bullish, and a short stock position is considered bearish.

10. A
A defined benefit plan favors older owner/employees and would provide the greatest retirement benefit to Pete.

11. B

The S&P index has systematic risk only. Systematic risk is also referred to as non-diversifiable risk. The other answers (non-systematic risk, diversifiable risk, and unsystematic risk) all refer to the same type of risk.

12. B

Class B mutual fund shares charge a back-end load.

13. C

Regulation A permits unregistered public offerings of up to $5 million of securities in any 12-month period.

14. B

The Customer Identification Program (CIP) is a requirement in which financial institutions need to verify the identity of individuals wishing to conduct financial transactions with them.

15. A

The book entry form of ownership allows an investor to own securities without a certificate.

16. D

The MSRB (Municipal Securities Rulemaking Board) has the mission of protecting investors, municipal entities, and the public interest by promoting a fair and efficient municipal market, regulating firms that engage in municipal securities and advisory activities, and promoting market transparency.

17. B

Mortgage REITs invest in loans secured by real estate.

18. C

A REMIC is a self-liquidating, flow-through entity that invests in real estate mortgages or mortgage-backed securities.

19. A

Equity REITs acquire ownership interests in commercial, industrial, and residential properties. Income is received from the rental of these properties.

20. C

According to FINRA Rule 3240, borrowing and lending arrangements between a Registered Investment Advisor and its customers requires the member firm to have a written policy in place.

21. A

Series EE bonds provide tax-exempt interest if the proceeds are used to pay for qualifying education expenses.

22. A

A bearer bond is a type of bond that is unregistered, with no record kept regarding the owner or transactions involving ownership.

23. C
Liquidity is the ability to sell or redeem an investment quickly and at a known price without incurring a significant loss of principal. Marketability is the speed and ease with which an investment may be bought or sold.

24. C
To be considered an accredited investor, net worth must exceed $1,000,000, either alone or together with a spouse, excluding the value of the person's primary residence.

25. C
For ADRs, banks collect money in their local currency and then convert to U.S. dollars. ADRs are traded on secondary exchanges and represent ownership interest in foreign securities denominated in U.S. dollars. They are issued by banks in foreign countries.

26. B
A warrant may be attached to new debt or preferred issues to make the issues more attractive to buyers. A difference between rights and warrants is their lifespan. Rights usually expire within a few weeks, and warrants may continue without expiring for up to several years.

27. A
The Board of Governors is the governing body of FINRA and oversees the administration of its affairs and the promotion of its welfare, objectives, and purposes.

28. D
Preferred stock that does not have to pay missed dividends is considered noncumulative.

29. A
Securities Act Rule 144 permits the public resale of restricted or control securities if a number of conditions are met, including how long the securities are held, the way in which they are sold, and the amount that can be sold at any one time.

30. C
A flat yield curve generally indicates an economic slowdown. It occurs when there is little difference between short-term and long-term yields for debt instruments of the same credit quality.

31. D
Regulation S-P requires firms to have policies and procedures addressing the protection of customer information and records. This regulation also requires firms to provide initial and annual privacy notices to customers describing information sharing policies.

32. B
According to the Telephone Consumer Protection Act, solicitors are prohibited from calling residences before 8 a.m. and after 9 p.m. local time.

33. B
Churning describes the illegal practice of excessive buying and selling of securities in a customer's account without considering the customer's investment goals. Its primary goal is to generate commissions that benefit the broker.

34. D

The two main types of mutual fund prospectuses are the statutory prospectus and the summary prospectus.

35. B

Treasury notes are sold in minimum denominations of $100.

36. B

Treasury STRIPS are always issued at a discount to par, like zero-coupon bonds.

37. A

The Howey test is the result of the U.S. Supreme Court case, Securities and Exchange Commission v. W. J. Howey Co. from 1946. It is used to determine whether an instrument qualifies as an "investment contract" for the purposes of the Securities Act of 1933.

38. C

Only Government National Mortgage Association certificates (Ginnie Maes) are backed by the full faith and credit of the U.S. government.

39. A

Consolidated tape refers to the high-speed electronic system that reports the latest price and volume data on sales of exchange-listed stocks.

40. B

A bond's call provision may be included in a bond agreement, and it allows the debtor to pay off the debt after a specific period of time at a predetermined price. It protects the issuer from declines in interest rates. If a bond is callable it will cause an investor's required rate of return to be higher.

41. C

In order to be eligible to make a traditional IRA contribution, an individual must be younger than age 70 ½ by the end of the taxable year.

42. D

The Federal Open Market Committee (FOMC) consists of 12 members and holds 8 regularly scheduled meetings per year. It reviews economic and financial conditions and determines the appropriate stance of monetary policy.

43. D

The stages of money laundering, in the correct order, are placement, layering, integration.

44. D

The Securities Investor Protection Act of 1970 regulates brokerage firms.

45. C

The Investment Company Act of 1940 regulates mutual funds.

46. A

The Securities Act of 1933 regulates new securities.

47. B

The Securities Exchange Act of 1934 regulates existing securities.

48. B

If interest rates decline following a bond issue, a sinking-fund provision will allow an issuing company to reduce the interest rate risk of its bonds as it replaces a portion of the existing debt with lower yielding bonds.

49. B

Interest rate risk is the risk that, as interest rates rise, bond prices will fall. Interest rate risk is measured by a bond's duration.

50. A

A stabilizing bid is the process in which an underwriter intervenes in the secondary market by placing a bid for securities at or below the offering price. The goal is to protect the price from dropping if there is a lack of initial interest for a new issue.

51. A

A due diligence meeting is an internal meeting between the officials of an organization that will be issuing securities and members of the syndicate that will be distributing them. The meeting is held after the registration of a new security with the SEC, but before the registration's effective date.

52. C

The annual report on Form 10-K provides a comprehensive overview of a company's business and financial condition and includes audited financial statements.

53. B

Types of municipal bonds include general obligation bonds, private activity bonds, and revenue bonds.

54. A

Roth IRA contributions are made with after-tax dollars and grow tax-free. Alex will not owe taxes when he takes the distribution.

55. B

If corporate bonds are selling at a significant premium, then newly issued bonds are selling with lower coupons. The corporations are likely to call their bonds and replace them with lower coupon bonds.

56. D

The IARD is an electronic filing system that facilitates investment adviser registration, exempt reporting adviser filing, regulatory review, and the public disclosure information of registered investment adviser firms and individuals.

57. C

The Insider Trading and Securities Fraud Enforcement Act of 1988 established the policies and procedures commonly referred to as a "Chinese wall."

58. A

In general, the smaller a security's bid-ask spread, the better its liquidity.

59. D

Sovereign debt is issued by a national government in a foreign currency in order to finance the issuing country's growth and development.

60. C

The two broad categories of defined contribution plans are profit sharing plans and pension plans.

61. B

The Dow Jones Industrial Average is an index comprised of 30 industrial companies.

62. C

The Federal Reserve determines the minimum margin requirement for investment accounts.

63. D

Regarding municipal bonds, a good faith deposit is the small amount of money, usually less than 5% of an issue, that underwriters give to the issuer in exchange for the right to place part of the issue.

64. C

Unlike a 529 plan, funds in a UGMA/UTMA account do not grow tax-deferred. However, the funds in the UGMA/UTMA account do not need to be used to pay for education expenses. The custodian, typically the minor's parent, does not own the assets in the account. Once the account is set up, it's considered to be an irrevocable gift.

65. B

A currency transaction report (CTR) must be filed by U.S. financial institutions for each deposit, withdrawal, exchange of currency, or other payment to the institution which involves a transaction in currency of more than $10,000.

66. B

A spread is the simultaneous purchase of one option and the sale of another option on the same side or position within the market. For example, purchasing a call option and selling a call option on the same stock at the same time is a spread.

67. A

A collar is a technique used to protect an investor's gain in a long position of stock. Specifically, an investor purchases a put option to protect against a decline in the value of an underlying stock, and sells a call option to generate premium income to cover the cost of the put option premium.

68. D

In a protective put, an investor purchases a put option while holding shares of an underlying stock from a previous purchase.

69. C

A straddle is the simultaneous purchase of a call option and a put option on the same stock at the same time.

70. A

The smaller a bond's coupon, the greater its relative price fluctuation. The smaller a bond's coupon, the lower its reinvestment risk.

71. A

A 401(k) plan is a qualified plan, and a 403(b) plan is not a qualified plan.

72. D

$R_t = (P_t - P_{t-1} + D_t) \div P_{t-1}$
$R_t = (\$173 - \$184 + \$4.25) \div \$184 = -0.0367 = -3.67\%$

73. D

A corporate insider is defined as a director or senior officer of a company, as well as any person or entity that beneficially owns more than 10% of a company's voting shares.

74. C

The typical limit on the term of a loan from a qualified retirement plan is 5 years.

75. A

The Securities Acts Amendments of 1975 gave authority to the Municipal Securities Rule-making Board (MSRB).

PRACTICE EXAM 3

QUESTIONS

1. All but which of the following statements are correct regarding bonds and preferred stock?

   A. If a company declares bankruptcy, bondholders are repaid before preferred stock shareholders.
   B. Preferred stocks pay dividends; bonds pay interest.
   C. Bonds are subject to greater interest rate risk than preferred stock.
   D. Neither bond interest nor preferred stock dividends qualify for capital gains treatment.

2. Which of the following is correct regarding a pre-emptive right?

   A. It is also referred to as a "subscription right" or a "subscription privilege."
   B. It is an obligation for existing shareholders to purchase new shares of stock before they are offered to the public.
   C. Exercising a pre-emptive right can cause dilution.
   D. All of the above are correct.

3. Which of the following is a characteristic of American Depository Receipts (ADRs)?

   A. ADRs trade once per day like mutual funds.
   B. ADR holders receive foreign tax credits for income tax paid to a foreign country.
   C. ADR dividends are declared in U.S. dollars.
   D. ADRs allow domestic securities to be traded in foreign countries.

4. Which of the following is the measure of a company's earnings per share if all convertible securities were exercised and converted to common stock?

   A. Converted earnings per share
   B. Conversion ratio per share
   C. Diluted earnings per share
   D. Price/earnings per share

5. Which of the following is the voice of state securities agencies responsible for efficient capital formation and grass-roots investor protection in the U.S.? Their fundamental mission is to protect consumers who purchase securities or investment advice, and their jurisdiction extends to a wide variety of issuers and intermediaries who offer and sell securities to the public.

   A. NAIC
   B. NASAA
   C. NASD
   D. SIPC

6. Which of the following is defined as the benefit provided to an asset manager by a broker-dealer as a result of commissions generated from financial transactions executed by the broker-dealer?

    A. 12b-1 compensation
    B. Administrative compensation
    C. Hard-dollar compensation
    D. Soft-dollar compensation

7. Which of the following is/are correct regarding interest paid from municipal bonds?

    (1) Interest paid from municipal bonds is not taxed by the federal government.
    (2) Interest paid from municipal bonds is never taxable at the state level.

    A. (1) only
    B. (2) only
    C. Both (1) and (2) are correct.
    D. Neither (1) or (2) are correct.

8. All but which of the following are correct regarding investment adviser representatives (IARs)?

    A. Every investment advisory firm must have at least one IAR registered to the firm.
    B. An IAR can be a dual registrant of multiple firms in some states only.
    C. There are currently no continuing education requirements for IARs.
    D. An IAR does not need to be registered to an RIA firm in order to conduct investment advisory business.

9. Which of the following is an investor protection requirement that obligates a broker-dealer to exercise reasonable care to execute a customer's order in a way to obtain the most advantageous terms for the customer?

    A. Best execution
    B. Price execution
    C. Price improvement
    D. Prudent man rule

10. A health savings account (HSA) allows the account holder to set aside money on a/an _____ basis to pay for _____ medical expenses.

    A. after-tax, qualified
    B. after-tax, unqualified
    C. pre-tax, qualified
    D. pre-tax, unqualified

11. Which of the following is the central banking system of the United States?

    A. Federal Reserve
    B. FOMC
    C. U.S. Mint
    D. U.S. Treasury

12. If an investor's brokerage firm goes out of business and is a member of the SIPC, then the investor's cash and securities held by the firm may be protected up to _____, including a _____ limit for cash.

    A. $500,000, $250,000
    B. $500,000, $500,000
    C. $1,000,000, $250,000
    D. $1,000,000, $500,000

13. All but which of the following are characteristics of defined contribution plans?

    A. Employer contributions are defined.
    B. The employee assumes the risk of investment performance.
    C. The employer assumes the risk of pre-retirement inflation.
    D. Benefits cannot be provided for past service.

14. A "penny stock" is an equity security that trades below:

    A. $0.05.
    B. $0.50.
    C. $1.00.
    D. $5.00.

15. The FDIC maintains stability and public confidence in the nation's financial system by doing all but which of the following?

    A. Insuring deposits.
    B. Managing receiverships.
    C. Examining and supervising financial institutions for safety, soundness, and consumer protection.
    D. Setting minimum standards for voluntarily established pension and health plans.

16. Which of the following provides clearing, settlement, risk management, central counterparty services, and a guarantee of completion for certain transactions for virtually all broker-to-broker trades involving equities, corporate and municipal debt, ADRs, ETFs, and UITs?

    A. ATC
    B. NSCC
    C. OCC
    D. TRACE

17. Which of the following must be filed for each of the first three fiscal quarters of a company's fiscal year, and includes unaudited financial statements and provides a continuing view of the company's financial position during the year?

    A. Form ADV
    B. Form 8-K
    C. Form 10-K
    D. Form 10-Q

18. According to SEC Rule 506(b), private placements may be sold to how many accredited and non-accredited investors?

    A. An unlimited number of accredited investors and up to 35 non-accredited investors.
    B. An unlimited number of accredited investors and up to 100 non-accredited investors.
    C. A total of 35 accredited and non-accredited investors.
    D. A total of 100 investors, of which 35 can be non-accredited.

19. Kappa Inc., a C Corp, had a profitable year and has extra money to invest. The owners would like to maximize the after-tax income to the corporation. Which of the following investments would best help them achieve their goal?

    A. Value stocks
    B. Preferred stock
    C. Municipal bonds
    D. Highly-rated corporate bonds

20. Which of the following regulations contains rules providing exemptions from the registration requirements under the Securities Act of 1933?

    A. Regulation A
    B. Regulation G
    C. Regulation T
    D. Regulation U

21. Which of the following describes the maturities of Treasury bills, Treasury notes, and Treasury bonds?

    A. Treasury notes have maturities of 10 years or more.
    B. Treasury bills have maturities of 1 year or more.
    C. Treasury bonds have maturities greater than 10 years.
    D. All of the above are correct.

22. Which of the following is a set of documents, including a prospectus, which a company must file with the SEC pursuant to the Securities Act of 1933 before it proceeds with a public offering?

    A. Prospectus statement
    B. Red herring
    C. Registration statement
    D. Tombstone ad

23. If the yield curve is _____, then the spread between yields of short-term and long-term bonds is _____.

    A. flattening, decreasing
    B. flattening, increasing
    C. steepening, decreasing
    D. steepening, increasing

For questions 24 – 27, match the form of dividend with the description that follows. Use only one answer per blank. Answers may be used more than once or not at all.

    A. Stock dividend
    B. Credit dividend
    C. Ordinary dividend
    D. Qualified dividend
    E. Constructive dividend
    F. Liquidating dividend
    G. Tax dividend

24. ____ A distribution made by a corporation that is paid as additional shares of stock rather than cash.

25. ____ A type of dividend to which capital gains tax rates are applied.

26. ____ Normally a disguised dividend, such as a below-market shareholder loan.

27. ____ A payment to shareholders that exceeds the company's retained earnings; payment is made from capital rather than earnings.

28. Which of the following are backed by the full faith and credit of the government issuing the bonds and are repaid through taxes collected by the government body?

    A. General obligation bonds
    B. Moral obligation bonds
    C. Private purpose bonds
    D. Revenue bonds

29. All but which of the following are correct regarding Electronic Communication Networks (ECNs)?

    A. They are a type of alternative trading system (ATS).
    B. They trade unlisted stocks and other non-exchange-traded products.
    C. Unlike dark pools, ECNs display orders in the consolidated quote stream.
    D. ECNs are required to register with the SEC as broker-dealers.

30. Which of the following was established by FINRA as an integrated audit trail of order, quote, and trade information for all National Market System stocks and OTC equity securities?

    A. ACATS
    B. EMMA
    C. NBBO
    D. OATS

31. Which of the following is correct regarding the selling price of Treasury STRIPS?

    A. They are sold at a discount from face value.
    B. They are sold at a premium to face value.
    C. They are sold at face value.
    D. They are sold at either a discount or premium to face value.

32. All but which of the following are correct regarding the IARD?

    A. It was developed according to the requirements of its sponsors, the SEC and NASAA.
    B. Its database helps promote uniformity through the use of common forms, and efficiency through a paperless environment.
    C. It is to investment advisers what the CRD is to broker-dealers.
    D. All of the above are correct.

33. Which of the following describes bonds that have a legal claim to specific assets in the event of default, insolvency, or liquidation?

    A. Debenture bonds
    B. Indenture bonds
    C. Secured bonds
    D. Unsecured bonds

34. As bond interest rates _____, bond duration _____.

    A. decrease, decreases
    B. decrease, increases
    C. increase, increases
    D. increase, is unchanged

35. If an investor expects a large decrease in the stock market 60 days from today, she can take advantage of the change by doing which of the following?

(1) Buying S&P 500 index calls
(2) Buying S&P 500 index puts
(3) Selling S&P 500 index calls
(4) Selling S&P 500 index puts

A. (1) and (3) only
B. (1) and (4) only
C. (2) and (3) only
D. (2) and (4) only

36. Which of the following acts regulates the organization of companies, including mutual funds, that engage primarily in investing, reinvesting, and trading in securities? The act is designed to minimize conflicts of interest that arise in these complex operations.

A. Securities Exchange Act of 1934
B. Trust Indenture Act of 1939
C. Investment Company Act of 1940
D. Uniform Securities Act of 1956

37. Which of the following are established by states to provide other governmental entities (e.g., cities, counties, and school districts) with a short-term investment vehicle to purchase shares or units in an investment portfolio?

A. GICs
B. HOLDRs
C. LGIPs
D. UITs

38. Which of the following is/are correct regarding open-end mutual funds?

(1) Open-end mutual funds sell at their net asset value (NAV).
(2) Open-end mutual funds have a fixed capital structure.

A. (1) only
B. (2) only
C. Both (1) and (2) are correct.
D. Neither (1) or (2) are correct.

39. All but which of the following are correct regarding unit investment trusts (UITs)?

A. Units may be bought or sold on the secondary market.
B. Upon termination of a UIT, any remaining securities in the trust will be sold and proceeds will be paid to investors.
C. Units are sold to investors for a minimum cost of $100,000.
D. They typically have low fees and expenses.

40. All but which of the following are types of annuity settlement options?

    A. Extended term
    B. Installment refund
    C. Life with period certain
    D. Single life

For questions 41 – 43, match the type of risk with the description that follows. Use only one answer per blank. Answers may be used more than once or not at all.

    A. Business risk
    B. Tax risk
    C. Financial risk
    D. Market risk
    E. Credit risk
    F. Country risk

41. ___ The risk associated with a company's decision to use debt as part of its capital structure.

42. ___ The possibility that a bond issuer will default.

43. ___ The risk inherent in company operations.

44. An investor sold short 25 shares of Omikron stock at a price of $98.50 per share. She also simultaneously placed a "good-till-cancelled, stop 102, limit 107 buy" order. Excluding transaction costs, what is the investor's maximum potential loss?

    A. $208.50
    B. $210.50
    C. $212.50
    D. $214.25

45. Which of the following regulations sets out certain requirements for lenders, other than securities brokers and dealers, who extend credit secured by margin stock?

    A. Regulation S
    B. Regulation T
    C. Regulation U
    D. Regulation W

46. Which of the following terms refers to a broker using securities in his or her possession, but owned by a customer, as collateral to raise a loan to cover a short position?

    A. Recapitalization
    B. Recollateralization
    C. Rehypothecation
    D. Securitization

For questions 47 – 49, match the economic policy with the description that follows. Use only one answer per blank. Answers may be used more than once or not at all.

    A. Expansionary policy
    B. Contractionary policy

47. ___ Taxes increase

48. ___ Public spending increases

49. ___ Government borrowing decreases

50. Phil has owned his company, Beta Corporation, for 15 years. He is now 52 years old and plans to retire at age 64. He has five young employees and wants to establish a retirement plan that will provide him with the highest benefit. Assuming adequate cash flow, which of the following is the most suitable plan for Beta Corporation to establish?

    A. Age-based profit sharing plan
    B. Defined benefit plan
    C. Money purchase plan
    D. SIMPLE IRA

51. Which of the following are short-term, fixed-income securities that may be bought or sold in the open market at a market-determined price?

    A. ADRs
    B. Call options
    C. Eurodollars
    D. Negotiable CDs

52. Which of the following regulations governs the extension of credit by broker-dealers and controls the margin requirements for stock purchases?

    A. Regulation D
    B. Regulation S
    C. Regulation T
    D. Regulation U

53. Which of the following is the FINRA committee that reviews initial decisions rendered in FINRA disciplinary and membership proceedings? It may affirm, dismiss, modify, or reverse any finding, or remand the case for further proceedings.

    A. Board of Governors
    B. FINRA Disciplinary Council
    C. National Adjudicatory Council
    D. None of the above are correct.

54. To promote and enhance cyber security, a Registered Investment Advisor's Chief Compliance Officer should educate firm employees about which of the following fraudulent activities that involves obtaining financial or other confidential information from internet users, usually by sending an email that looks as though it has been sent by a legitimate organization? The email usually contains a link to a fake website that looks authentic.

    A. Phishing
    B. Spamming
    C. Spoofing
    D. Worming

55. Justin, age 58, contributes to his employer's 401(k). In 2018, he will contribute $24,500 to the plan through salary deferrals, and he would like to contribute to an IRA as well. If he is single and has an income of $250,000, the maximum IRA contribution that he can make is:

    A. $5,500 to a deductible IRA.
    B. $6,500 to a deductible IRA.
    C. $6,500 to a non-deductible IRA.
    D. $6,500 to a Roth IRA.

56. According to FINRA, which of the following elements must be addressed in a firm's business continuity plan relating to an emergency or significant business disruption?

    A. Alternate physical location of employees
    B. Communications with regulators
    C. Data backup and recovery
    D. All of the above are correct.

57. Which of the following represents the minimum price that a seller is willing to receive for a security?

    A. Ask price
    B. Bid price
    C. Call price
    D. NAV

58. Which of the following is a broker in the futures market who has a direct relationship with a client, but delegates the work of the floor operation and trade execution to another futures merchant?

    A. Carrying broker
    B. Clearing broker
    C. Executing broker
    D. Introducing broker

59. Which of the following are characteristics of Series EE bonds?

(1) They may be purchased for an amount equal to one-half of face value.
(2) They may be purchased for a minimum price of $25 for a $50 bond.
(3) The U.S. Treasury guarantees that an EE bond's value will double after 10 years.
(4) They may be purchased for a maximum price of $5,000 for a $10,000 bond.

A. (1) only
B. (1), (2), and (4) only
C. (2), (3), and (4) only
D. All of the above are correct.

60. Which of the following are permitted investments in an IRA?

A. A mutual fund that invests exclusively in a silver mining stock.
B. Gold coins minted in the U.S.
C. A real estate investment trust.
D. All of the above are correct.

61. Which of the following is the maximum civil penalty that can be imposed upon an individual who commits an insider trading violation?

A. The civil penalty may be an amount up to two times the profit gained or the loss avoided as a result of the insider trading violation.
B. The civil penalty may be an amount up to three times the profit gained or the loss avoided as a result of the insider trading violation.
C. The civil penalty may be an amount up to $50,000.
D. The civil penalty may be an amount up to $100,000.

62. TIPS are indexed to the rate of inflation as measured by which of the following?

A. Producer Price Index
B. Personal Consumption Expenditures Price Index
C. Implicit Price Deflator
D. Consumer Price Index

63. Which of the following is a type of debt security that repackages and directs the payments of principal and interest from a collateral pool to different types and maturities of securities?

A. CMO
B. GIC
C. REIT
D. UIT

64. Which of the following are basic provisions of a universal life insurance policy?

(1) Flexible death benefit
(2) Flexible premium
(3) Minimum guaranteed cash value
(4) Unbundled structure

A. (1) and (2) only
B. (2) and (3) only
C. (1), (2), and (4) only
D. (1), (3), and (4) only

65. If an individual contributes more to an IRA than is permitted, the excess contribution is subject to which of the following taxes?

A. 5% excise tax
B. 6% excise tax
C. 10% excise tax
D. 15% excise tax

66. An investment adviser will be deemed to have custody of client assets if which of the following apply?

A. The advisor has possession of client funds or securities and does not return them to the client within 3 days.
B. The advisor is authorized or permitted to withdraw client funds or securities.
C. The adviser has legal ownership or access to client funds or securities.
D. All of the above are correct.

67. An investor purchases two puts. The first is a September Theta put at $35, underlying currently selling at $37. The second is a November Delta put at $28, underlying currently selling at $25. Ignoring transaction costs, what is the value of the options?

A. Theta: −$2; Delta: $3
B. Theta: $0; Delta: −$3
C. Theta: $0; Delta: $3
D. Theta: $2; Delta: $3

68. Which of the following is a system that automates and standardizes procedures for the transfer of assets in a customer account from one brokerage firm and/or bank to another?

A. ACATS
B. ECN
C. TRACE
D. WIRE

69. A nonexempt unregistered security may be sold through which of the following?

    A. Common stock
    B. IPO
    C. Mutual fund
    D. Private placement

70. Which of the following is correct regarding a bond's coupon rate?

    A. It is the stated annual interest rate that will be paid each period for the term of a bond.
    B. It is stated as a percentage of the current market price of a bond.
    C. A 5% coupon bond will pay $50 each semiannual period for a $1,000 bond.
    D. A bond's coupon rate is also its yield to maturity (YTM).

71. Which of the following is correct regarding non-systematic risk?

    A. It includes risks such as tax risk and financial risk.
    B. An investor who owns five growth stocks can reduce non-systematic risk by adding a value stock to her portfolio.
    C. It is the risk associated with a particular security or company.
    D. All of the above are correct.

72. Which of the following is correct regarding commercial paper?

    A. It has a maturity of 270 days or less.
    B. It's issued in denominations of $1,000 or more.
    C. It does not act as a viable substitute for short-term bank financing.
    D. It has less default risk than Treasury bills.

73. Which of the following is an electronic quotation listing of the bid and asked prices of OTC stocks that do not meet the requirements to be listed on the NASDAQ stock-listing system?

    A. ECN
    B. Instinet
    C. OTC Bulletin Board
    D. OTC Quotation System

74. Which of the following acts is designed to provide greater deterrence and punishment for people trading on material non-public information, and to improve detection of other perceived market abuses?

    A. Securities Act Amendments of 1975
    B. Insider Trading and Securities Fraud Enforcement Act of 1988
    C. National Securities Market Improvement Act of 1996
    D. Sarbanes-Oxley Act of 2002

75. The Regulatory Element of FINRA's Continuing Education Program requires all registered individuals to complete a computer-based training session within _____ days of the second anniversary of their initial registration date, and every three years thereafter.

A. 30
B. 60
C. 120
D. 180

ANSWER KEY

1. C
Preferred stock does not have a fixed maturity date. Therefore, it has unlimited interest rate risk. If a company declares bankruptcy, bondholders are repaid before preferred stock shareholders. Preferred stocks pay dividends; bonds pay interest. Neither bond interest nor preferred stock dividends qualify for capital gains treatment.

2. A
A pre-emptive right is also referred to as a "subscription right" or a "subscription privilege." It is a right, but not an obligation for existing shareholders to exercise, and it prevents dilution among existing shareholders.

3. B
ADRs allow for the trading of international securities in domestic countries. They trade throughout the day, and their dividends are declared in local currencies and paid in U.S. dollars. ADR holders receive foreign tax credits for income tax paid to a foreign country.

4. C
Diluted earnings per share is the measure of a company's earnings per share if all convertible securities were exercised and converted to common stock.

5. B
The NASAA (North American Securities Administrators Association) is the voice of state securities agencies responsible for efficient capital formation and grass-roots investor protection in the U.S. Their fundamental mission is to protect consumers who purchase securities or investment advice, and their jurisdiction extends to a wide variety of issuers and intermediaries who offer and sell securities to the public.

6. D
Soft-dollar compensation is defined as the benefit provided to an asset manager by a broker-dealer as a result of commissions generated from financial transactions executed by the broker-dealer.

7. A
Interest paid from municipal bonds is not taxed by the federal government. The bond interest may also be tax-exempt by various states if certain requirements are met.

8. D
In order to conduct investment advisory business, an investment adviser representative (IAR) must be registered to an RIA firm, and every investment advisory firm must have at least one IAR. An IAR can be a dual registrant of multiple firms in some states only. There are currently no continuing education requirements for IARs.

9. A
"Best execution" is an investor protection requirement that obligates a broker-dealer to exercise reasonable care to execute a customer's order in a way to obtain the most advantageous terms for the customer.

10. C
A health savings account (HSA) allows the account holder to set aside money on a pre-tax basis to pay for qualified medical expenses.

11. A
The Federal Reserve is the central banking system of the United States.

12. A
If an investor's brokerage firm goes out of business and is a member of the SIPC, then the investor's cash and securities held by the firm may be protected up to $500,000, including a $250,000 limit for cash.

13. C
In a defined contribution plan, employer contributions are defined, and benefits cannot be provided for past service. The employee assumes the risk of investment performance and pre-retirement inflation.

14. D
A "penny stock" is an equity security that trades below $5.

15. D
The FDIC maintains stability and public confidence in the nation's financial system by insuring deposits, managing receiverships, and examining and supervising financial institutions for safety, soundness, and consumer protection. ERISA, not the FDIC, sets minimum standards for voluntarily established pension and health plans.

16. B
The NSCC (National Securities Clearing Corporation) provides clearing, settlement, risk management, central counterparty services, and a guarantee of completion for certain transactions for virtually all broker-to-broker trades involving equities, corporate and municipal debt, ADRs, ETFs, and UITs.

17. D
Form 10-Q must be filed for each of the first three fiscal quarters of a company's fiscal year. It includes unaudited financial statements and provides a continuing view of the company's financial position during the year.

18. A
According to SEC Rule 506(b), private placements may be sold to an unlimited number of accredited investors and up to 35 non-accredited investors.

19. B
Corporate investors in preferred stock can generally deduct 70% of the dividends they receive.

20. A
Regulation A contains rules providing exemptions from the registration requirements under the Securities Act of 1933.

21. C
Treasury bills have maturities of 1 year or less.
Treasury notes have maturities of 10 years or less.
Treasury bonds have maturities greater than 10 years.

22. C
A registration statement is a set of documents, including a prospectus, which a company must file with the SEC pursuant to the Securities Act of 1933 before it proceeds with a public offering.

23. A
If the yield curve is flattening, then the spread between yields of short-term and long-term bonds is decreasing.

24. A
Stock dividends are distributions by a corporation that are paid as additional shares of stock rather than cash.

25. D
A qualified dividend is a type of dividend to which capital gains tax rates are applied.

26. E
A disguised dividend, such as a below-market shareholder loan, is considered to be a constructive dividend.

27. F
A payment to shareholders that exceeds the company's retained earnings is a liquidating dividend. The payment is made from capital rather than earnings.

28. A
General obligation bonds are backed by the full faith and credit of the government issuing the bonds and are repaid through taxes collected by the government body.

29. B
Electronic Communication Networks (ECNs) are a type of alternative trading system (ATS) that trades listed stocks and other exchange-traded products. Unlike dark pools, ECNs display orders in the consolidated quote stream. ECNs are required to register with the SEC as broker-dealers.

30. D
OATS (Order Audit Trail System) was established by FINRA as an integrated audit trail of order, quote, and trade information for all National Market System stocks and OTC equity securities.

31. A
Treasury STRIPS are sold at a discount from face value.

32. D

The IARD was developed according to the requirements of its sponsors, the SEC and NASAA. Its database helps promote uniformity through the use of common forms, and efficiency through a paperless environment. It is to investment advisers what the CRD is to broker-dealers.

33. C

Secured bonds have a legal claim to specific assets in the event of default, insolvency, or liquidation.

34. B

As bond interest rates decrease, bond duration increases.

35. C

If an investor expects a large decrease in the stock market 60 days from today, she can take advantage of the change by buying S&P 500 index puts and selling S&P 500 index calls.

36. C

The Investment Company Act of 1940 regulates the organization of companies, including mutual funds, that engage primarily in investing, reinvesting, and trading in securities. The act is designed to minimize conflicts of interest that arise in these complex operations.

37. C

LGIPs (local government investment pools) are established by states to provide other governmental entities (e.g., cities, counties, and school districts) with a short-term investment vehicle to purchase shares or units in an investment portfolio.

38. A

Open-end mutual funds sell at their net asset value (NAV) and do not have a fixed capital structure.

39. C

Unit investment trusts (UITs) are sold to investors for a typical cost of $1,000. Units may be bought or sold on the secondary market, and upon termination of a UIT, any remaining securities in the trust will be sold and proceeds will be paid to investors. They typically have low fees and expenses.

40. A

The annuity settlement options are cash, single life, life with period certain, joint-and-survivor, and installment refund.

41. C

Financial risk is the risk associated with a company's decision to use debt as part of its capital structure.

42. E

Credit risk is the possibility that a bond issuer will default.

43. A
Business risk is the risk inherent in company operations.

44. C
($107 – $98.50) × 25 shares = $212.50

45. C
Regulation U sets out certain requirements for lenders, other than securities brokers and dealers, who extend credit secured by margin stock.

46. C
Rehypothecation refers to a broker using securities in his or her possession, but owned by a customer, as collateral to raise a loan to cover a short position.

47. B
Contractionary policy is characterized by taxes increasing, public spending decreasing, and government borrowing decreasing.

48. A
Expansionary policy is characterized by taxes decreasing, public spending increasing, and government borrowing increasing.

49. B
Contractionary policy is characterized by taxes increasing, public spending decreasing, and government borrowing decreasing.

50. B
The defined benefit plan would provide the greatest benefit to Phil because he has five younger employees, and defined benefit plans favor older owner/employees. Of the other options listed, the age-based profit sharing plan is a valid consideration. However, the question says to assume adequate cash flow in the business. Profit sharing plans would benefit from unstable cash flow because contributions must only be substantial and re-curring. The best answer is the defined benefit plan.

51. D
Negotiable CDs are short-term, fixed-income securities that may be bought or sold in the open market at a market-determined price.

52. C
Regulation T governs the extension of credit by broker-dealers and controls the margin requirements for stock purchases.

53. C
The National Adjudicatory Council (NAC) is the FINRA committee that reviews initial de-cisions rendered in FINRA disciplinary and membership proceedings. It may affirm, dis-miss, modify, or reverse any finding, or remand the case for further proceedings.

54. A

Phishing is a fraudulent activity that involves obtaining financial or other confidential information from internet users, usually by sending an email that looks as though it has been sent by a legitimate organization. The email usually contains a link to a fake website that looks authentic.

55. C

Because Justin is an active participant in an employer-sponsored retirement plan, he is subject to an AGI phaseout of $63,000 to $73,000 in 2018. Because his income is above the phaseout range, he is not eligible to make a deductible IRA contribution. His AGI is too high to contribute to a Roth IRA, as well. The Roth IRA AGI phaseout is $120,000 to $135,000 in 2018.

56. D

According to FINRA, a firm's business continuity plan must address the following relating to an emergency or significant business disruption: An alternate physical location of employees, communications with regulators, and data backup and recovery.

57. A

The ask price represents the minimum price that a seller is willing to receive for a security.

58. D

An introducing broker is a broker in the futures market who has a direct relationship with a client, but delegates the work of the floor operation and trade execution to another futures merchant.

59. B

Series EE bonds may be purchased for an amount equal to one-half of face value. The minimum price is $25 for a $50 bond, and the maximum price is $5,000 for a $10,000 bond. At a minimum, the U.S. Treasury guarantees that an EE bond's value will double after 20 years.

60. D

All of the items listed are permitted investments in an IRA. These include a mutual fund that invests exclusively in a silver mining stock, gold coins minted in the U.S., and a real estate investment trust (REIT).

61. B

The civil penalty may be an amount up to three times the profit gained or the loss avoided as a result of the insider trading violation.

62. D

TIPS (treasury inflation-protected securities) are indexed to the rate of inflation as measured by the Consumer Price Index (CPI).

63. A

A CMO (collateralized mortgage obligation) is a type of debt security that repackages and directs the payments of principal and interest from a collateral pool to different types and maturities of securities.

64. C
Universal life insurance policies have a flexible premium and death benefit, and are said to have an "unbundled structure." They do not have a minimum guaranteed cash value.

65. B
If an individual contributes more to an IRA than is permitted, the excess contribution is subject to a 6% excise tax.

66. D
An investment advisor will be deemed to have custody of client assets if the advisor has possession of client funds or securities and does not return them to the client within 3 days, the advisor is authorized or permitted to withdraw client funds or securities, or the adviser has legal ownership or access to client funds or securities.

67. C
The Theta option is out-of-the-money, therefore its value is $0. The value of the Delta option is $28 – $25 = $3.

68. A
The Automated Client Account Transfer Service (ACATS) is a system that automates and standardizes procedures for the transfer of assets in a customer account from one brokerage firm and/or bank to another.

69. D
A nonexempt unregistered security may be sold through a private placement.

70. A
A bond's coupon rate is the stated annual interest rate that will be paid each period for the term of a bond. It is stated as a percentage of the face value of the bond.

71. D
Non-systematic risk is the risk associated with a particular security or company. It includes risks such as tax risk and financial risk. An investor who owns five growth stocks can reduce non-systematic risk by adding a value stock to her portfolio.

72. A
Commercial paper has a maturity of 270 days or less and is issued in denominations of $100,000 or more.

73. C
The OTC Bulletin Board is an electronic quotation listing of the bid and asked prices of OTC stocks that do not meet the requirements to be listed on the NASDAQ stock-listing system.

74. B
The Insider Trading and Securities Fraud Enforcement Act of 1988 is designed to provide greater deterrence and punishment for people trading on material non-public information, and to improve detection of other perceived market abuses.

75. C

The Regulatory Element of FINRA's Continuing Education Program requires all registered individuals to complete a computer-based training session within 120 days of the second anniversary of their initial registration date, and every three years thereafter.

PRACTICE EXAM 4

QUESTIONS

1. Expansionary policy is characterized by which of the following?

    A. Decreasing transfer payments
    B. Increasing public spending
    C. Increasing taxes
    D. All of the above are correct.

2. Which of the following is an order to sell a security at or above a specified price?

    A. Sell limit order
    B. Sell market order
    C. Sell top order
    D. None of the above are correct.

3. Which of the following is the formula to calculate an investment's taxable equivalent yield?

    A. Taxable equivalent yield = Tax-free yield ÷ (1 − Marginal tax rate)
    B. Taxable equivalent yield = Tax-free yield ÷ (1 + Marginal tax rate)
    C. Taxable equivalent yield = (1 − Marginal tax rate) ÷ Tax-free yield
    D. Taxable equivalent yield = (1 + Marginal tax rate) ÷ Tax-free yield

4. Which of the following forms is the "Uniform Application for Securities Industry Registration or Transfer," which representatives of broker-dealers, investment advisers, or issuers of securities must fill out in order to become registered in the appropriate jurisdictions?

    A. Form U4
    B. Form U5
    C. Form U6
    D. Form U7

5. The Trust Indenture Act of 1939 prohibits bond issues over _____ from being offered for sale without a formal agreement signed by both the bond issuer and the bondholder that fully discloses the details of the issue.

    A. $1 million
    B. $5 million
    C. $10 million
    D. $15 million

6. All but which of the following are characteristics of defined benefit plans?

    A. Employer contributions vary.
    B. Participant benefits vary.
    C. The employer assumes the investment risk.
    D. They favor older employees.

7. Which of the following are primary issuers of individual bonds?

    (1) Local government
    (2) U.S. government
    (3) An agency of the U.S. government
    (4) Corporations

    A. (1) and (4) only
    B. (1), (2), and (3) only
    C. (2), (3), and (4) only
    D. All of the above are correct.

8. Which of the following allows a firm to file one registration statement covering several issues of the same security? The securities can then be sold over a period of several years.

    A. Deferred registration
    B. Omitting registration
    C. Shelf registration
    D. Statutory registration

9. Firms must retain trade blotters containing all purchases and sales of securities for at least _____ years, and they must keep copies of confirmations for _____ years. For the first _____ years, these records must be kept in an easily accessible location.

    A. 3, 2, 2
    B. 4, 3, 2
    C. 5, 4, 3
    D. 6, 3, 2

10. Which of the following lists the assets provided in the correct order from most liquid to least liquid?

    (1) Real estate
    (2) Treasury bills
    (3) Limited partnership
    (4) Investment-grade corporate bonds

    A. 2, 1, 4, 3
    B. 4, 2, 3, 1
    C. 3, 1, 4, 2
    D. 2, 4, 1, 3

11. All but which of the following is another name for a balance sheet?

    A. Net worth statement
    B. Statement of assets and liabilities
    C. Statement of cash flows
    D. Statement of financial position

12. Which of the following mutual fund share classes will charge investors a front-end load?

    A. Class A shares
    B. Class B shares
    C. Class C shares
    D. Class D shares

13. All but which of the following are correct regarding advertising activities engaged in by a Registered Investment Advisor?

    A. Securities laws and rules prohibit performance advertising.
    B. Advertisements may not use or refer to testimonials.
    C. A testimonial refers to any statement of a client's experience or endorsement.
    D. All of the above are correct.

14. Blue sky laws are classified as which of the following?

    A. Federal-based laws
    B. International-based laws
    C. Municipal-based laws
    D. State-based laws

15. Which of the following was the self-regulatory organization for the over-the-counter market, and is now part of FINRA?

    A. NAC
    B. NASAA
    C. NASD
    D. NYSE

16. Investment risk is defined as which of the following?

    A. The chance that an investment's actual return will be greater or less than its expected return.
    B. The chance that an investment's actual return will equal its expected return.
    C. The chance that an investment's actual return will be less than its expected return.
    D. None of the above are correct.

17. Which of the following acts is credited with forming the Municipal Securities Rulemaking Board (MSRB)?

    A. Securities Investor Protection Act of 1970
    B. Securities Act Amendments of 1975
    C. Uniform Prudent Investors Act of 1994
    D. National Securities Market Improvement Act of 1996

18. To be considered an accredited investor, earned income must exceed _____ (or _____ together with a spouse) in each of the prior two years, and must be reasonably expected to occur for the current year.

    A. $200,000, $300,000
    B. $300,000, $400,000
    C. $400,000, $500,000
    D. $500,000, $600,000

19. Buying a _____ and selling a _____ are both bearish strategies.

    A. put, call
    B. put, put
    C. call, call
    D. call, put

20. Which of the following is/are correct regarding closed-end mutual funds?

    (1) Closed-end mutual funds may issue new shares when an individual buys existing shares.
    (2) Closed-end mutual funds may sell at a premium or discount to their net asset value.

    A. (1) only
    B. (2) only
    C. Both (1) and (2) are correct.
    D. Neither (1) or (2) are correct.

21. Which of the following is the world's largest equity derivatives clearing organization? By acting as guarantor, they ensure that the obligations of the contracts that they clear are fulfilled.

    A. AMBAC
    B. NASDAQ
    C. NSCC
    D. OCC

22. Which of the following is correct regarding open market operations?

    A. It is a tool used by the Federal Reserve to implement monetary policy.
    B. It is conducted by the Trading Desk at the Federal Reserve Bank of New York.
    C. The authority to conduct open market operations is found in Section 14 of the Federal Reserve Act.
    D. All of the above are correct.

23. If real GDP declined last quarter, how many more consecutive quarters of decline would be needed to be classified as an economic recession?

    A. 1 quarter
    B. 2 quarters
    C. 3 quarters
    D. 4 quarters

For questions 24 – 26, select the word that best completes the bond relationship provided. Use only one answer per blank. Answers may be used more than once or not at all.

    A. More
    B. Less

24. ___ Lower-coupon bonds are _____ affected by interest rate changes than higher-coupon bonds.

25. ___ The shorter a bond's term to maturity, the _____ its potential for relative price fluctuation.

26. ___ Long-term bonds are _____ affected by interest rate changes than short-term bonds.

27. Which of the following government agencies are responsible for monitoring qualified retirement plan rules and eligibility?

    A. ERISA and the IRS
    B. ERISA and the PBGC
    C. IRS and the Department of Labor
    D. IRS and the PBGC

28. To calculate core inflation, which of the following categories are excluded from the calculation?

    A. Food and energy prices
    B. Food and utilities
    C. Healthcare and energy prices
    D. Technology and utilities

29. Which of the following is correct regarding Keynesian economics?

    A. It is considered a "demand-side" theory that focuses on changes in the economy over the long run.
    B. It is considered a "demand-side" theory that focuses on changes in the economy over the short run.
    C. It is considered a "supply-side" theory that focuses on changes in the economy over the long run.
    D. It is considered a "supply-side" theory that focuses on changes in the economy over the short run.

30. Prices for goods and services will _____ when their demand exceeds their supply.

    A. deflate
    B. inflate
    C. stagflate
    D. remain unchanged

31. An investor who owns 5% cumulative preferred stock will receive a semiannual dividend of:

    A. $0.25 per share.
    B. $0.50 per share.
    C. $2.50 per share.
    D. $5.00 per share.

32. Which of the following is the National Securities Clearing Corporation's core engine that acts as the central counterparty for clearance and settlement for virtually all broker-to-broker equity, corporate, and municipal bond trading in the United States? It settles trades from the nation's major exchanges and nets those transactions to one security position per member per day.

    A. CNS System
    B. DTCC System
    C. OATS System
    D. RTRS System

33. According to FINRA guidelines, broker-dealers who conduct general securities business and carry customer funds and securities must meet a _____ minimum net capital requirement.

    A. $5,000
    B. $25,000
    C. $50,000
    D. $250,000

34. Which of the following is correct regarding IRA contributions?

    A. IRA contributions made above the maximum annual limit are subject to a 10% nondeductible excise tax.
    B. A nonworking divorced person, age 40, who receives alimony may contribute to an IRA the lesser of the maximum contribution limit or 100% of the alimony received.
    C. An employee who makes voluntary contributions to a 401(k) plan is not considered an active participant for the purpose of making IRA contributions.
    D. An employee participating in a 457 plan is considered an active participant for the purpose of making IRA contributions.

35. All but which of the following are correct regarding Treasury notes?

    A. They are issued by the U.S. Treasury Department.
    B. They have maturities of 10 years or less.
    C. They make variable interest payments on a semiannual basis.
    D. They are taxed at the federal level only.

36. When an investment company puts home mortgages or other loans into a pool and then sells securities representing shares of the pool, the securities sold are referred to as which of the following?

    A. Asset-backed securities
    B. Dark pools
    C. Derivative-backed securities
    D. Unit investment trusts

37. Which of the following refers to taking a loss on a bond and replacing it with a substantially different bond to avoid triggering the wash sale rule?

    A. Bond conversion
    B. Bond spread
    C. Bond swap
    D. Bond yield

38. An investor purchased a call option for $3.00. The option has a strike price of $37.00, and the stock is currently valued at $36.00. The call option would cost $2.50 if purchased today. Ignoring transaction costs, what is the value of the option?

    A. –$0.50
    B. $0
    C. $1.00
    D. $2.00

39. All but which of the following are characteristics of REITs?

    A. Losses cannot be passed through to investors to deduct personally.
    B. REIT shareholders are subject to double taxation.
    C. REITs can be purchased in small denominations.
    D. All of the above are correct.

40. Which of the following entities is subject to double taxation?

    A. C Corp
    B. S Corp
    C. LLC
    D. Partnership

41. What is the maximum contribution a donor can make in a single year to a 529 plan if the gift tax annual exclusion is $15,000? Assume the donor has not made previous contributions to a 529 plan.

    A. $15,000
    B. $30,000
    C. $75,000
    D. $105,000

42. Christine purchased 100 shares of Alpha stock for $50 per share. At the end of two years, she sold the shares for $70 per share. In the first year, the stock did not pay a dividend. In the second year, the stock paid a $3 dividend. What was the holding period return of Christine's investment?

    A. 23%
    B. 26%
    C. 32%
    D. 46%

43. All but which of the following are characteristics of tangible assets, such as collectibles?

    A. They do not have a strong secondary market.
    B. They are not subject to significant government regulation.
    C. They are marketable.
    D. They lack liquidity.

44. Which of the following insures the interest and principal payments for municipal bonds and other public finance debt obligations?

    A. AMBAC
    B. DOL
    C. FDIC
    D. PBGC

45. Which of the following is/are correct regarding profit sharing plans?

    (1) Profit sharing plans are a type of defined contribution pension plan.
    (2) The minimum funding standard requires the employer to make an annual contribution.

    A. (1) only
    B. (2) only
    C. Both (1) and (2) are correct.
    D. Neither (1) or (2) are correct.

46. The Russell 2000 measures the performance of _____ U.S. stocks.

    A. small-cap
    B. mid-cap
    C. large-cap
    D. blended

For questions 47 – 50, determine if the exchange described qualifies as a 1035 exchange. Use only one answer per blank. Answers may be used more than once or not at all.

    A. 1035 exchange
    B. Not a 1035 exchange

47. ___ A life insurance policy exchanged for a life insurance policy.

48. ___ An annuity exchanged for an annuity.

49. ___ An annuity exchanged for a life insurance policy.

50. ___ A life insurance policy exchanged for an annuity.

51. Which of the following are correct regarding Roth IRAs?

    (1) Contributions to a Roth IRA can be made at any age.
    (2) Contributions to a Roth IRA must be made before age 70 ½.
    (3) A Roth IRA owner is not required to take a minimum distribution during his or her lifetime.
    (4) Roth IRA contributions may be deducted in limited circumstances.

    A. (1) and (3) only
    B. (2) and (3) only
    C. (1), (3), and (4) only
    D. (2), (3), and (4) only

52. Which of the following are characteristics of a zero-coupon bond?

    (1) It does not make periodic interest payments throughout the term of the bond.
    (2) It has significant reinvestment risk because no payments are made until the bond matures.
    (3) It requires taxes to be paid on accrued interest each year, even though no interest is received.
    (4) The duration of a zero-coupon bond is less than its term to maturity.

    A. (1) and (3) only
    B. (2) and (4) only
    C. (1), (2), and (3) only
    D. (2), (3), and (4) only

53. Which of the following is correct regarding certificates of deposit (CDs)?

    A. They are short-term securities that may be bought or sold in the open market at a market-determined price.
    B. They typically invest in high-quality, short-term investments, such as commercial paper, Treasury bills, and money market funds.
    C. They are known as "time deposits."
    D. The financial institution typically pays a variable rate of interest for the term of the CD.

54. Client information must be kept confidential unless which of the following circumstances apply?

    A. The information is needed to establish an advisory or brokerage account.
    B. The information is required in response to proper legal process.
    C. The information is in connection with a civil dispute between the adviser and the client.
    D. All of the above are correct.

55. According to the Telephone Consumer Protection Act, companies must maintain do-not-call lists reflecting the names of customers who have requested to be excluded from telemarketing, and those requests must be honored for how many years?

    A. 1 year
    B. 2 years
    C. 5 years
    D. 7 years

56. Which of the following is the illegal trading practice of manipulating the market by buying and selling a security to create the illusion of high trading activity and to attract other traders who may increase the price?

    A. Capping and pegging
    B. Front running
    C. Painting the tape
    D. Trading ahead

57. Lauren purchased a bond with a face value of $1,000 and a coupon rate of 4.5%. Her effective tax rate is 25%. If the risk-free rate is 4%, and coupon payments are made semiannually, what is the periodic interest payment?

    A. $16.88, paid twice per year.
    B. $22.50, paid twice per year.
    C. $45.00, paid once per year.
    D. $45.00, paid twice per year.

58. Which of the following SEC regulations require member firms that offer or maintain covered accounts to develop and implement written identity theft prevention programs?

    A. Regulation BB
    B. Regulation CF
    C. Regulation FD
    D. Regulation S-ID

For questions 59 – 62, match the type of stock with the description that follows. Use only one answer per blank. Answers may be used more than once or not at all.

    A. Cyclical stocks
    B. Defensive stocks

59. ___ Pharmaceutical companies

60. ___ Automobiles

61. ___ Airlines

62. ___ Railroads

63. Which of the following are prohibited investments in an IRA?

    (1) U.S. minted gold coins
    (2) Antiques
    (3) U.S. stamps
    (4) Art work

    A. (1) only
    B. (1), (2), and (4) only
    C. (2), (3), and (4) only
    D. All of the above are correct.

64. Which of the following describes actions taken by the Federal Reserve and their effect on the money supply?

    (1) If the Federal Reserve sells government securities, it receives money in return, which increases the money supply.
    (2) If the Federal Reserve sells government securities, it is considered contractionary policy.

    A. (1) only
    B. (2) only
    C. Both (1) and (2) are correct.
    D. Neither (1) or (2) are correct.

65. Which of the following yield curves results from similar yields among Treasury notes, Treasury bonds, and Treasury bills?

    A. Flat yield curve
    B. Inverted yield curve
    C. Negative yield curve
    D. Steep yield curve

66. A _____ is issued by a governmental body to finance a specific project. It is not backed by the full faith and credit of the issuing body.

    A. general obligation bond
    B. multi-purpose bond
    C. private activity bond
    D. revenue bond

67. Puts are an option to _____ a specified number of shares of stock during a specified period at a specified price. A buyer of a put option expects the price of the underlying stock to _____.

    A. buy, fall
    B. buy, rise
    C. sell, fall
    D. sell, rise

68. Which of the following is correct regarding the relationship between an investment's real return and nominal return?

    (1) Real return is an investment's rate of return after adjusting for inflation.
    (2) Nominal return is an investment's rate of return without adjusting for inflation.

    A. (1) only
    B. (2) only
    C. Both (1) and (2) are correct.
    D. Neither (1) or (2) are correct.

69. Dr. Jones, age 29, recently opened a successful dental practice. She's concerned that her young employees will leave for a more experienced dental practice once they're fully trained. In order to retain her young employees, which retirement plan should Dr. Jones adopt?

    A. Cash balance plan
    B. Defined benefit plan
    C. Money purchase plan
    D. Target benefit plan

70. Which of the following is referred to as the "know your customer" rule, which states that a customer's situation must be suitable for any investment being made?

    A. Securities Act Rule 144
    B. Securities Act Rule 405
    C. Securities Act Rule 433
    D. Securities Act Rule 506

71. A diversified mutual fund cannot own more than _____ of the shares of a given company or more than _____ of fund assets in a given investment.

    A. 5%, 5%
    B. 10%, 5%
    C. 20%, 10%
    D. 20%, 20%

72. Which of the following is the maximum criminal fine for a non-natural person (such as an entity whose securities are publicly traded) who commits an insider trading violation?

    A. $5 million
    B. $10 million
    C. $25 million
    D. $50 million

73. Which of the following is correct regarding the SEC's guidance on the "testimonial rule" and social media?

    A. Testimonials were originally addressed in Rule 206(4)-1(a)(1) of the Investment Advisers Act of 1940.
    B. Advisers are allowed to select favorable testimonials to include on their websites only if client names are kept confidential.
    C. Advisers are allowed to select favorable testimonials to include on their websites only if they receive permission from the clients, and they post each client's full name.
    D. None of the above are correct.

74. According to Regulation D, firms may sell private placements to how many non-accredited investors in a 12-month period?

    A. 0
    B. 25
    C. 35
    D. 50

75. **Which of the following is a type of bond offered as a tranche class of some CMOs, according to a sinking-fund schedule?**

A. General obligation bond
B. Planned amortization class (PAC) bond
C. Targeted amortization class (TAC) bond
D. Zero-coupon bond

ANSWER KEY

1. B
Expansionary policy is characterized by decreasing taxes, increasing public spending, and increasing government borrowing.

2. A
A sell limit order is an order to sell a security at or above a specified price.

3. A
Taxable equivalent yield = Tax-free yield ÷ (1 – Marginal tax rate)

4. A
Form U4 is the "Uniform Application for Securities Industry Registration or Transfer," which representatives of broker-dealers, investment advisers, or issuers of securities must fill out in order to become registered in the appropriate jurisdictions.

5. B
The Trust Indenture Act of 1939 prohibits bond issues over $5 million from being offered for sale without a formal agreement signed by both the bond issuer and the bondholder that fully discloses the details of the issue.

6. B
In a defined benefit plan, employer contributions can vary but participant benefits are fixed. The employer assumes the investment risk, and they tend to favor older employees.

7. D
The primary issuers of individual bonds are local government, state government, U.S. government, an agency of the U.S. government, and corporations.

8. C
Shelf registrations allows a firm to file one registration statement covering several issues of the same security. The securities can then be sold over a period of several years.

9. D
Firms must retain trade blotters containing all purchases and sales of securities for at least 6 years, and they must keep copies of confirmations for 3 years. For the first 2 years, these records must be kept in an easily accessible location.

10. D
The assets ranked from most liquid to least liquid are Treasury bills, investment-grade corporate bonds, real estate, and the limited partnership.

11. C
A balance sheet can also be referred to as a net worth statement, statement of assets and liabilities, and statement of financial position.

12. A
Class A mutual fund shares charge a front-end load.

13. A

Advertisements by a Registered Investment Advisor may not use or refer to testimonials, which refers to any statement of a client's experience or endorsement. Securities laws and rules do not prohibit performance advertising.

14. D

Blue sky laws are classified as state-based laws.

15. C

The NASD (National Association of Securities Dealers) was the self-regulatory organization for the over-the-counter market and is now part of FINRA.

16. C

Investment risk is the chance that an investment's actual return will be less than its expected return.

17. B

The Securities Act Amendments of 1975 created the Municipal Securities Rulemaking Board (MSRB).

18. A

To be considered an accredited investor, earned income must exceed $200,000 (or $300,000 together with a spouse) in each of the prior two years, and must be reasonably expected to occur for the current year.

19. A

Buying a put and selling a call are both bearish strategies.

20. B

Closed-end mutual funds may sell at a premium or discount to their net asset value. Only open-end mutual funds may issue new shares when an individual buys existing shares.

21. D

The OCC (Options Clearing Corporation) is the world's largest equity derivatives clearing organization. By acting as guarantor, they ensure that the obligations of the contracts that they clear are fulfilled.

22. D

Open market operations is a tool used by the Federal Reserve to implement monetary policy. It is conducted by the Trading Desk at the Federal Reserve Bank of New York, and the authority to conduct open market operations is found in Section 14 of the Federal Reserve Act.

23. A

2 quarters – 1 quarter = 1 quarter

An economic recession is defined as a decline in real GDP for 2 or more consecutive quarters.

24. A

Lower-coupon bonds are more affected by interest rate changes than higher-coupon bonds. Lower-coupon bonds have more price volatility.

25. B

The shorter a bond's term to maturity, the less its potential for relative price fluctuation. Long-term bonds have more price volatility.

26. A

Long-term bonds are more affected by interest rate changes than short-term bonds. Long-term bonds have more price volatility.

27. C

The two government agencies responsible for monitoring qualified retirement plan rules and eligibility are the IRS and the Department of Labor.

28. A

To calculate core inflation, food and energy prices are excluded from the calculation.

29. B

Keynesian economics is considered a "demand-side" theory that focuses on changes in the economy over the short run.

30. B

Prices for goods and services will inflate when their demand exceeds their supply.

31. C

An investor who owns 5% cumulative preferred stock will receive a semiannual dividend of $2.50 per share.

32. A

The CNS (Continuous Net Settlement) System is the National Securities Clearing Corporation's core engine that acts as the central counterparty for clearance and settlement for virtually all broker-to-broker equity, corporate, and municipal bond trading in the United States. It settles trades from the nation's major exchanges and nets those transactions to one security position per member per day.

33. D

According to FINRA guidelines, broker-dealers who conduct general securities business and carry customer funds and securities must meet a $250,000 minimum net capital requirement.

34. B

The nondeductible excise tax for over-contributing to an IRA is 6%, not 10%. An employee who makes voluntary contributions to a 401(k) plan is considered an active participant. However, an employee participating in a 457 plan is not an active participant. A nonworking divorced person, age 40, who receives alimony may contribute to an IRA the lesser of the maximum contribution limit or 100% of the alimony received.

35. C

Treasury notes are issued by the U.S. Treasury Department and have maturities of 10 years or less. They have fixed interest payments that are made semiannually to maturity, and they are taxed at the federal level only.

36. A
When an investment company puts home mortgages or other loans into a pool and then sells securities representing shares of the pool, the securities sold are referred to as asset-backed securities.

37. C
A bond swap refers to taking a loss on a bond and replacing it with a substantially different bond to avoid triggering the wash sale rule.

38. B
The call option is out-of-the-money because the strike price ($37.00) exceeds the market price ($36.00). Therefore, the value of the option is $0.

39. B
REITs can be purchased in small denominations, and losses cannot be passed through to investors to deduct personally. REIT shareholders are not subject to double taxation.

40. A
A C Corp is subject to double taxation. Earnings are taxed once at the entity level and again at the individual level once distributions have occurred.

41. C
$5 \times \$15,000 = \$75,000$
A donor may contribute a total of five gift tax annual exclusion amounts on a one-time basis every five years to a 529 plan.

42. D
$HPR = [(\$7,000 + \$300) - \$5,000] \div \$5,000 = 0.46 = 46\%$

43. C
Collectibles lack marketability and liquidity. They do not have a strong secondary market and they're not subject to significant government regulation.

44. A
AMBAC (American Municipal Bond Assurance Corporation) insures the interest and principal payments for municipal bonds and other public finance debt obligations.

45. D
A profit sharing plan is a type of defined contribution plan other than a pension plan. Contributions must be substantial and recurring, but are not required annually.

46. A
The Russell 2000 measures the performance of small-cap U.S. stocks.

47. A
A life insurance policy exchanged for a life insurance policy is a permitted 1035 exchange.

48. A
An annuity exchanged for an annuity is a permitted 1035 exchange.

49. B

An annuity exchanged for a life insurance policy is not a permitted 1035 exchange.

50. A

A life insurance policy exchanged for an annuity is a permitted 1035 exchange.

51 A

Contributions to a Roth IRA can be made at any age and are never deductible. A Roth IRA owner is not required to take a minimum distribution during his or her lifetime.

52. A

A zero-coupon bond does not make periodic interest payments, however it requires taxes to be paid on accrued interest each year. A zero-coupon bond has no reinvestment risk, and its duration is equal to its term to maturity.

53. C

Certificates of deposit (CDs) are known as "time deposits." They are deposits made with a bank for a specified period of time.

54. D

Client information must be kept confidential unless the information is needed to establish an advisory or brokerage account, the information is required in response to proper legal process, or the information is in connection with a civil dispute between the adviser and the client.

55. C

According to the Telephone Consumer Protection Act, companies must maintain do-not-call lists reflecting the names of customers who have requested to be excluded from tele-marketing. Such requests must be honored for 5 years.

56. C

Painting the tape is the illegal trading practice of manipulating the market by buying and selling a security to create the illusion of high trading activity and to attract other traders who may increase the price.

57. B

Periodic interest payment = ($1,000 × 0.045) ÷ 2 = $22.50

58. D

Regulation S-ID requires member firms that offer or maintain covered accounts to de-velop and implement written identity theft prevention programs.

59. B

Pharmaceutical companies are defensive stocks.

60. A

Automobiles are cyclical stocks.

61. A

Airlines are cyclical stocks.

62. A
Railroads are cyclical stocks.

63. C
Collectibles that are prohibited investments in IRAs include antiques, stamps, art work, rugs, metals, gems, stamps, and coins. There is an exception for U.S. minted gold coins.

64. B
If the Federal Reserve sells government securities, it receives money in return, which reduces the money supply. This is considered contractionary policy.

65. A
A flat yield curve results from similar yields among Treasury notes, Treasury bonds, and Treasury bills.

66. D
A revenue bond is issued by a governmental body to finance a specific project. It is not backed by the full faith and credit of the issuing body. Instead, debts are repaid from revenue generated from the project that was financed.

67. C
Puts are an option to sell a specified number of shares of stock during a specified period at a specified price. A buyer of a put option expects the price of the underlying stock to fall.

68. C
Real return is an investment's rate of return after adjusting for inflation. Nominal return is an investment's rate of return without adjusting for inflation.

69. C
The cash balance plan, defined benefit plan, and target benefit plan all favor older employees. Money purchase plans guarantee a contribution will be made each year and will help Dr. Jones achieve her goal of retaining her young employees.

70. B
Securities Act Rule 405 is referred to as the "know your customer" rule, which states that a customer's situation must be suitable for any investment being made.

71. B
A diversified mutual fund cannot own more than 10% of the shares of a given company or more than 5% of fund assets in a given investment.

72. C
The maximum criminal fine for a non-natural person (such as an entity whose securities are publicly traded) who commits an insider trading violation is $25 million.

73. A
Testimonials were originally addressed in Rule 206(4)-1(a)(1) of the Investment Advisers Act of 1940. In general, client testimonials are not permitted to be included on adviser websites and social media.

74. C

According to Regulation D, firms may sell private placements to 35 non-accredited investors in a 12-month period.

75. C

A targeted amortization class (TAC) bond is a type of bond offered as a tranche class of some CMOs, according to a sinking-fund schedule.

PRACTICE EXAM 5

QUESTIONS

1. All but which of the following are correct regarding the stock market trading pattern known as "sector rotation"?

   A. It involves shifting investments from one sector of the economy to another.
   B. It is a passive investment strategy, similar to indexing.
   C. It assumes that sector performance is correlated to the business cycle.
   D. It can be expensive to implement because of the potential costs associated with extensive trading activity.

2. Which of the following are correct regarding exchange-traded funds (ETFs)?

   (1) Unlike mutual funds, investors can buy and sell ETFs throughout the trading day.
   (2) ETFs can be bought on margin or sold short.
   (3) There is never a transaction fee to buy or sell an ETF.
   (4) ETFs have low management fees compared to mutual funds.

   A. (3) only
   B. (4) only
   C. (1), (2), and (3) only
   D. (1), (2), and (4) only

3. Which of the following is a manipulative trading activity that is designed to prevent the price of a security from rising?

   A. Capping
   B. Front running
   C. Painting the tape
   D. Pegging

4. Distributions from a 401(k) plan following separation from service after age _____ are not subject to the _____ premature distribution penalty.

   A. 50, 10%
   B. 50, 15%
   C. 55, 10%
   D. 55, 15%

5. Which of the following is a fee deducted from a mutual fund's assets to pay for marketing and distribution costs associated with operating the fund?

   A. Accounting fee
   B. Custodial fee
   C. Transfer agent fee
   D. 12b-1 fee

6. Which of the following elements of FINRA's Continuing Education Program requires broker-dealers to establish a formal training program to keep covered registered persons updated on job and product-related subjects?

A. Compliance Element
B. Firm Element
C. Regulatory Element
D. Regulatory and Firm Elements

7. A variable life insurance policy will pay benefits that vary according to which of the following?

A. The flexibility of premiums paid.
B. The value of underlying investments.
C. The variability of the mortality factor.
D. All of the above are correct.

8. Which of the following allow investors to aggregate their own holdings as well as the holdings of certain related parties, such as spouses and children, toward achieving the investment thresholds at which breakpoint discounts become available?

A. Rights of accumulation
B. Rights of conversion
C. Rights of deferment
D. Rights of indenture

9. Hybrid REITs combine features of which of the following?

A. Equity REITs and commodity REITs
B. Equity REITs and mortgage REITs
C. Mortgage REITs and commodity REITs
D. None of the above are correct.

10. Which of the following is an agreement between the issuer of a security and its underwriters stating that the underwriters are responsible for any unsold portion of the issue? This transfers the risk of the unsold portion of the issue from the issuer to the underwriters.

A. Best efforts underwriting
B. Standard underwriting
C. Standby underwriting
D. Subscription underwriting

11. Which of the following represents the maximum price that a buyer is willing to pay for a security?

    A. Ask price
    B. Bid price
    C. Call price
    D. NAV

12. A retirement plan is _____ if more than 60% of total plan benefits are in favor of key employees.

    A. ERISA certified
    B. discriminatory
    C. illegal
    D. top heavy

13. Which of the following is a broker that offers clearing, settlement, and custodial services to other brokers, and enables them to provide full service to their clients without incurring the sizable costs of running a back office?

    A. Carrying broker
    B. Clearing broker
    C. Executing broker
    D. Introducing broker

14. Which of the following is the first prospectus released for a new issue, and is intended to solicit indications of interest? It does not contain the new issue's price, and it is subject to change.

    A. Pink sheet
    B. Red herring
    C. Shelf registration
    D. Tombstone ad

15. Which of the following is correct regarding the interest paid by Treasury STRIPS?

    A. They pay interest monthly.
    B. They pay interest semiannually.
    C. They pay interest annually.
    D. They do not pay interest.

16. Buying a _____ and selling a _____ are both bullish strategies.

    A. call, call
    B. call, put
    C. put, call
    D. put, put

17. All companies, foreign and domestic, are required to file registration statements, periodic reports, and other forms electronically through which of the following? Consumers can then access and download this information for free.

   A. CRD
   B. EDGAR
   C. IARD
   D. NSCC

18. If a corporation is required to pay unpaid dividends from prior years before paying a dividend to common stockholders, the stock is considered to be:

   A. accumulated preferred stock.
   B. convertible stock.
   C. cumulative preferred stock.
   D. preferred stock.

19. Which of the following yield curves results from short-term debt instruments having a higher yield than long-term debt instruments of the same credit quality?

   A. Flat yield curve
   B. Inverted yield curve
   C. Normal yield curve
   D. Steep yield curve

20. A call is an option to _____ a specified number of shares of stock during a specified period at a specified price. A buyer of a call option expects the price of the underlying stock to _____.

   A. buy, fall
   B. buy, rise
   C. sell, fall
   D. sell, rise

21. The individuals, groups, and entities, such as terrorists and narcotics traffickers, designated under programs that are not country-specific, are collectively known as _____. Their assets are blocked and U.S. persons are generally prohibited from dealing with them.

   A. FTOs
   B. ITNs
   C. SDNs
   D. SSTs

22. Which of the following forms must companies file with the SEC to announce certain material events or corporate changes that shareholders should be made aware of?

    A. Form 8-K
    B. Form 10-K
    C. Form 10-Q
    D. Form I-9

23. Which of the following is the process through which the state takes ownership of property that is, or is believed to be, abandoned or unclaimed?

    A. Defeasement
    B. Escheatment
    C. Estoppel
    D. Indemnification

For questions 24 – 30, match the economic indicator with the description that follows. Use only one answer per blank. Answers may be used more than once or not at all.

    A. Leading economic indicator
    B. Lagging economic indicator

24. ___ Change in consumer sentiment

25. ___ Average prime rate charged by banks

26. ___ Change in the Consumer Price Index (CPI)

27. ___ Orders for durable goods

28. ___ Average duration of unemployment

29. ___ Change in money supply

30. ___ Housing starts

31. A mutual fund with a high turnover rate will require _____ active management and will typically charge _____ expenses.

    A. less, higher
    B. less, lower
    C. more, higher
    D. more, lower

32. The standard deviation of an investment portfolio must be _____ the weighted average of the standard deviation of returns of the individual securities.

    A. equal to
    B. greater than
    C. less than
    D. less than or equal to

33. For a defined contribution plan, annual contributions to an employee's account are limited to the lesser of _____ of compensation or _____ in 2018.

    A. 20%, $18,500
    B. 20%, $24,500
    C. 25%, $55,000
    D. 25%, $220,000

34. Which of the following is/are correct regarding registered bonds and bearer bonds?

    (1) A registered bond is registered with the corporation or organization that issued the bond, and coupon payments are made to the owner of record.
    (2) A bearer bond can be transferred like cash, and coupon payments are made to the person who holds the bond.

    A. (1) only
    B. (2) only
    C. Both (1) and (2) are correct.
    D. Neither (1) or (2) are correct.

35. Which of the following is an investment strategy entered into to reduce or offset the risk of adverse price movements in a security by taking an offsetting position in another investment?

    A. Arbitrage
    B. Derivative
    C. Option
    D. None of the above are correct.

36. Assume that an investor wants to dollar cost average into Delta mutual fund by making quarterly purchases over a two-year period. If the total amount to be invested is $48,000, then how much will be invested each quarter if the fund's NAV increases by a total of 10% over the two-year period?

    A. $6,000
    B. $6,600
    C. $8,000
    D. $8,800

37. Which of the following is a type of bond secured by both a defined source of revenue (other than property taxes) and the full faith and credit or taxing power of an issuer?

A. Debenture bond
B. Double-barreled bond
C. General obligation bond
D. Subordinate bond

38. Which of the following is the maximum criminal fine for an individual who commits an insider trading violation?

A. $1 million
B. $5 million
C. $10 million
D. $15 million

39. Stock in direct investment plans, Treasury securities purchased directly from the U.S. Department of the Treasury, and recently issued municipal bonds are held in which of the following forms?

A. Book entry form
B. Issue entry form
C. Record entry form
D. Register entry form

40. Which of the following accounts is most suitable to hold a zero-coupon bond?

A. IRA
B. Joint taxable account
C. Payable on death account
D. Totten trust

41. Which of the following regulations governs private placement exemptions?

A. Regulation A
B. Regulation D
C. Regulation T
D. Regulation U

42. Which of the following is an order to buy a stock at a price above the current market price?

A. Buy stop order
B. Buy limit order
C. Buy market order
D. None of the above are correct.

43. Which of the following is/are correct regarding a bond's interest rate and term to maturity?

(1) The lower a bond's interest rate, the lower its relative price fluctuation.
(2) The longer a bond's term to maturity, the greater its relative price fluctuation.

A. (1) only
B. (2) only
C. Both (1) and (2) are correct.
D. Neither (1) or (2) are correct.

44. Which of the following is/are correct regarding powers of attorney and powers of appointment?

(1) A power of attorney is a legal document created by an individual authorizing someone else to act on his or her behalf.
(2) A power of appointment is a power given to a donee allowing him or her to dispose of the donor's property by selecting one or more beneficiaries to receive the property.

A. (1) only
B. (2) only
C. Both (1) and (2) are correct.
D. Neither (1) or (2) are correct.

For questions 45 – 48, match the type of risk with the description that follows. Use only one answer per blank. Answers may be used more than once or not at all.

A. Systematic risk
B. Unsystematic risk

45. ___ Default risk

46. ___ Political risk

47. ___ Reinvestment risk

48. ___ Tax risk

49. Which of the following is a contract between an investor and an issuer in which the issuer guarantees payment of a stated sum to the investor at some set date in the future? In return for this future payment, the investor agrees to pay the issuer a set amount of money either as a lump sum or in periodic installments.

A. ETN
B. FAC
C. ISO
D. NQSO

50. If an investment is held for more than one year, the holding period return _____ the true investment return on an annual basis. If an investment is held for less than one year, the holding period return _____ the true investment return.

   A. correctly states, overstates
   B. overstates, correctly states
   C. overstates, understates
   D. understates, overstates

51. An investor purchased a share of Omikron stock for $90.00 and sold it for $95.50. If the total return was 7.50%, the dividend paid during the holding period was:

   A. $1.20.
   B. $1.25.
   C. $1.35.
   D. $1.40.

52. Which of the following is a type of mutual fund that invests only in the equity securities of companies located outside the U.S.?

   A. Aggressive growth fund
   B. Balanced fund
   C. Global fund
   D. International fund

53. The Dow Jones Industrial Average is a/an _____ average of _____ blue chip U.S. stocks.

   A. equal-weighted, 30
   B. equal-weighted, 500
   C. price-weighted, 30
   D. price-weighted, 500

54. Which of the following is/are correct regarding investment risk in a qualified retirement plan?

   (1) In a defined contribution plan, the employer bears the investment risk.
   (2) In a defined benefit plan, the employee bears the investment risk.

   A. (1) only
   B. (2) only
   C. Both (1) and (2) are correct.
   D. Neither (1) or (2) are correct.

55. Money in a Coverdell Education Savings Account (ESA) must be used by the time the beneficiary is _____ years of age.

    A. 18
    B. 21
    C. 24
    D. 30

The following information relates to questions 56 – 58.

A convertible bond is issued with a par value of $10,000. The bond is currently priced at $9,500, and the underlying share price is $200.

56. The conversion ratio of the bond is:

    A. 47.5:1.
    B. 50.0:1.
    C. 52.5:1.
    D. 55.5:1.

57. The conversion value of the bond is:

    A. $9,500.
    B. $9,700.
    C. $9,800.
    D. $10,000.

58. The conversion condition for the bond is:

    A. below parity.
    B. at parity.
    C. above parity.
    D. unknown.

59. All but which of the following are tiers of the NASDAQ?

    A. NASDAQ Capital Market
    B. NASDAQ Global Market
    C. NASDAQ Global Select Market
    D. NASDAQ International Equity Market

60. All but which of the following are characteristics of a SEP IRA?

    A. It is entirely owned by the participant.
    B. Plan loans are permitted.
    C. The contribution deadline to a SEP IRA is April 15, including extensions.
    D. The account balance is 100% vested at all times.

61. Which of the following is the formula to calculate an investment's public offering price (POP)?

A. POP = NAV ÷ Sales charge
B. POP = Sales charge ÷ NAV
C. POP = NAV + Sales charge
D. POP = NAV − Sales charge

62. An option that can be exercised at any time up to and including its expiration date is a/an _____ style option.

A. American
B. Asian
C. Australian
D. European

63. Which of the following are obligated to maintain a bid or offer at the National Best Bid or Offer (NBBO) in each of their assigned securities at least 10% of the trading day?

A. Certified Exchange Specialists
B. Designated Market Makers
C. Registered Floor Brokers
D. Supplemental Liquidity Providers

64. Which of the following rules addresses the registration and resale requirements for securities issued in a merger, consolidation, acquisition of assets, or reclassification of securities?

A. Securities Act Rule 145
B. Securities Act Rule 172
C. Securities Act Rule 238
D. Securities Act Rule 405

65. All but which of the following information is commonly found on an investment account statement?

A. Disclosures
B. Fees
C. Income summary
D. All of the above are correct.

66. If a portfolio has a beta of 1.0, what type of risk does the portfolio have?

A. Diversifiable risk
B. Non-systematic risk
C. Systematic risk
D. Both non-systematic and diversifiable risk

67. Which of the following is a model statute designed to guide each state in drafting its state securities laws? It was created by the National Conference of Commissioners on Uniform State Laws.

A. Maloney Act
B. Patriot Act
C. Uniform Prudent Investors Act
D. Uniform Securities Act

68. Which of the following will result if a distribution is taken from a health savings account (HSA) by an individual under age 65, and the distribution is not used to pay for qualified medical expenses?

A. The distribution is subject to ordinary income tax only.
B. The distribution is subject to ordinary income tax and a 10% penalty.
C. The distribution is subject to ordinary income tax and a 15% penalty.
D. The distribution is not subject to tax.

69. When a corporation files a registration with the SEC in an effort to sell shares to the public, the period of time between the filing of the registration statement and its effective date is referred to as the:

A. cooling-off period.
B. prospectus period.
C. registration period.
D. terminable interest period.

70. Which of the following is the FINRA-developed vehicle that facilitates the mandatory reporting of over-the-counter secondary market transactions in eligible fixed income securities? All broker-dealers who are FINRA member firms have an obligation to report transactions in corporate bonds to this vehicle under an SEC-approved set of rules.

A. ACT
B. AML
C. CTR
D. TRACE

71. All but which of the following are permitted to establish a 403(b) plan for its employees?

A. Federal government
B. Private school
C. Public school
D. State government

72. Which of the following is correct regarding IAR registration?

A. Individual registrations can be administered at the state level or federal level, depending on where the RIA firm is registered.
B. All individual registrations are administered at the federal level, regardless of whether the RIA firm is registered at the SEC or state level.
C. All individual registrations are administered at the state level, regardless of whether the RIA firm is registered at the SEC or state level.
D. None of the above are correct.

73. Which of the following is the oldest international investor protection organization and is an association of state securities administrators who are charged with the responsibility to protect consumers who purchase securities or investment advice? Its membership consists of administrators from the territories, districts, and states of the U.S., Mexico, and Canada.

A. NAIC
B. NASAA
C. NASD
D. NSCC

74. For the substantially equal periodic payment (SEPP) exception to apply for premature distributions from a retirement plan, payments must continue for _____ or until the participant is _____, whichever is longer.

A. 5 years, age 59 ½
B. 5 years, age 65
C. 10 years, age 59 ½
D. 10 years, age 65

75. Which of the following is a type of best efforts underwriting that only becomes effective when a minimum amount of securities have been sold? Once the minimum requirement has been met, the underwriter may then sell securities up to a specified level under the terms of the offering.

A. All or none underwriting
B. Market out underwriting
C. Mini-maxi underwriting
D. Standby underwriting

ANSWER KEY

1. B

Sector rotation involves shifting investments from one sector of the economy to another. It assumes that sector performance is correlated to the business cycle, and it can be expensive to implement because of the potential costs associated with extensive trading activity. It is an active investment strategy, not passive.

2. D

Unlike mutual funds, investors can buy and sell exchange-traded funds (ETFs) throughout the trading day. ETFs can be bought on margin or sold short, and they carry low management fees because they require very little active management. There is typically a transaction fee any time an ETF is bought or sold.

3. A

Capping is a manipulative trading activity that is designed to prevent the price of a security from rising.

4. C

Distributions from a 401(k) plan following separation from service after age 55 are not subject to the 10% premature distribution penalty.

5. D

The 12b-1 fee is deducted from a mutual fund's assets to pay for marketing and distribution costs associated with operating the fund.

6. B

The Firm Element of FINRA's Continuing Education Program requires broker-dealers to establish a formal training program to keep covered registered persons updated on job and product-related subjects.

7. B

A variable life insurance policy will pay benefits that vary according to the value of the underlying investments.

8. A

Rights of accumulation allow investors to aggregate their own holdings as well as the holdings of certain related parties, such as spouses and children, toward achieving the investment thresholds at which breakpoint discounts become available.

9. B

Hybrid REITs combine features of equity REITs and mortgage REITs.

10. C

Standby underwriting is an agreement between the issuer of a security and its underwriters stating that the underwriters are responsible for any unsold portion of the issue. This transfers the risk of the unsold portion of the issue from the issuer to the underwriters.

11. B

The bid price represents the maximum price that a buyer is willing to pay for a security.

12. D
A retirement plan is top heavy if more than 60% of total plan benefits are in favor of key employees. Certain rules and conditions apply to top-heavy plans.

13. A
A carrying broker offers clearing, settlement, and custodial services to other brokers, and enables them to provide full service to their clients without incurring the sizable costs of running a back office.

14. B
A red herring is the first prospectus released for a new issue and is intended to solicit indications of interest. It does not contain the new issue's price, and it is subject to change.

15. D
Treasury STRIPS do not pay interest prior to maturity.

16. B
Buying a call and selling a put are both bullish strategies.

17. B
All companies, foreign and domestic, are required to file registration statements, periodic reports, and other forms electronically through EDGAR (Electronic Data Gathering, Analysis, and Retrieval). Consumers can then access and download this information for free.

18. C
If a corporation is required to pay unpaid dividends from prior years before paying a dividend to common stockholders, the stock is considered to be cumulative preferred stock.

19. B
An inverted yield curve results from short-term debt instruments having a higher yield than long-term debt instruments of the same credit quality.

20. B
A call is an option to buy a specified number of shares of stock during a specified period at a specified price. A buyer of a call option expects the price of the underlying stock to rise.

21. C
The individuals, groups, and entities, such as terrorists and narcotics traffickers, designated under programs that are not country-specific, are collectively known as SDNs (Specially Designated Nationals). Their assets are blocked and U.S. persons are generally prohibited from dealing with them.

22. A
Companies must file Form 8-K with the SEC to announce certain material events or corporate changes that shareholders should be made aware of.

23. B
Escheatment is the process through which the state takes ownership of property that is, or is believed to be, abandoned or unclaimed.

24. A

A change in consumer sentiment is a leading economic indicator.

25. B

The average prime rate charged by banks is a lagging economic indicator.

26. B

A change in the Consumer Price Index (CPI) is a lagging economic indicator.

27. A

Orders for durable goods are a leading economic indicator.

28. B

The average duration of unemployment is a lagging economic indicator.

29. A

A change in the money supply is a leading economic indicator.

30. A

Housing starts are a leading economic indicator.

31. C

A mutual fund with a high turnover rate will require more active management and will typically charge higher expenses.

32. D

The standard deviation of an investment portfolio must be less than or equal to the weighted average of the standard deviation of returns of the individual securities. If the securities in a portfolio are perfectly correlated, then the standard deviation of the portfolio will be equal to the weighted average of the standard deviations of the individual securities within the portfolio. If the securities in a portfolio are not perfectly correlated, then the standard deviation of the portfolio will be less than the weighted average of the standard deviations of the individual securities making up the portfolio. By adding additional securities, the standard deviation of the portfolio can never increase.

33. C

For a defined contribution plan, annual contributions to an employee's account are limited to the lesser of 25% of compensation or $55,000 in 2018.

34. C

A registered bond is registered with the corporation or organization that issued the bond, and coupon payments are made to the owner of record. A bearer bond can be transferred like cash, and coupon payments are made to the person who holds the bond.

35. B

A derivative is an investment strategy entered into to reduce or offset the risk of adverse price movements in a security by taking an offsetting position in another investment.

36. A

$48,000 ÷ 8 quarters = $6,000 per quarter

With dollar cost averaging, a flat dollar amount is invested each period regardless of the underlying investment's performance.

37. B

A double-barreled bond is secured by both a defined source of revenue (other than property taxes) and the full faith and credit or taxing power of an issuer.

38. B

The maximum criminal fine for an individual who commits an insider trading violation is $5 million.

39. A

Stock in direct investment plans, Treasury securities purchased directly from the U.S. Department of the Treasury, and recently issued municipal bonds are held in book entry form.

40. A

Of the choices provided, an IRA is the most suitable account to hold a zero-coupon bond because the interest would be tax-deferred. If a zero-coupon bond were held in a taxable account, then tax would be due on the interest earned each year, even though no interest was paid to the bondholder.

41. B

Regulation D governs private placement exemptions.

42. A

A buy stop order is an order to buy a stock at a price above the current market price.

43. B

The lower a bond's interest rate, the greater its relative price fluctuation. The longer a bond's term to maturity, the greater its relative price fluctuation.

44. C

A power of attorney is a legal document created by an individual authorizing someone else to act on his or her behalf. A power of appointment is a power given to a donee allowing him or her to dispose of the donor's property by selecting one or more beneficiaries to receive the property.

45. B

Default risk is a type of unsystematic risk.

46. B

Political risk is a type of unsystematic risk.

47. A

Reinvestment risk is a type of systematic risk.

48. B
Tax risk is a type of unsystematic risk.

49. B
An FAC (face-amount certificate) is a contract between an investor and an issuer in which the issuer guarantees payment of a stated sum to the investor at some set date in the future. In return for this future payment, the investor agrees to pay the issuer a set amount of money either as a lump sum or in periodic installments.

50. C
If an investment is held for more than one year, the holding period return overstates the true investment return on an annual basis. If an investment is held for less than one year, the holding period return understates the true investment return.

51. B
$R_t = (P_t - P_{t-1} + D_t) \div P_{t-1}$
$0.075 = (\$95.50 - \$90.00 + D_t) \div \$90.00$
$D_t = \$1.25$

52. D
International mutual funds invest in the equity securities of companies located outside the U.S. Global mutual funds invest in both international and domestic companies.

53. C
The Dow Jones Industrial Average is a price-weighted average of 30 blue chip U.S. stocks.

54. D
In a defined contribution plan, the employee bears the investment risk. In a defined benefit plan, the employer bears the investment risk.

55. D
Money in a Coverdell Education Savings Account (ESA) must be used by the time the beneficiary is 30 years of age.

56. B
Conversion ratio = Par value $\div$ Underlying share price
Conversion ratio = $\$10,000 \div \$200 = 50:1$

57. D
Conversion value = Underlying share price $\times$ Conversion ratio
Conversion value = $\$200 \times 50 = \$10,000$

58. C
Because the current price of the convertible bond is $9,500, the conversion value is greater than the bond's price, or above parity.

59. D
The NASDAQ Capital Market, NASDAQ Global Market, and NASDAQ Global Select Market are tiers of the NASDAQ.

60. B
A SEP IRA is entirely owned by the participant, and the account balance is 100% vested at all times. The contribution deadline to a SEP IRA is April 15, including extensions. Plan loans are not permitted from a SEP IRA.

61. C
The formula to calculate an investment's public offering price is: POP = NAV + Sales charge

62. A
An option that can be exercised at any time up to and including its expiration date is an American style option.

63. D
Supplemental Liquidity Providers are obligated to maintain a bid or offer at the National Best Bid or Offer (NBBO) in each of their assigned securities at least 10% of the trading day.

64. A
Securities Act Rule 145 addresses the registration and resale requirements for securities issued in a merger, consolidation, acquisition of assets, or reclassification of securities.

65. D
According the FINRA, the information commonly found on an investment account statement includes contact information, clearing firm information, account summary, income summary, fees, account activity, margin, portfolio detail, and disclosures.

66. C
A portfolio with a beta of 1.0 will move in the same direction as the overall stock market. Therefore, the portfolio has only market risk, also known as systematic risk.

67. D
The Uniform Securities Act was created by the National Conference of Commissioners on Uniform State Laws, and is a model statute designed to guide each state in drafting its state securities laws.

68. B
Distributions from a health savings account (HSA) that are not used to pay for qualified medical expenses are subject to ordinary income tax and a 10% penalty. The penalty is waived if the individual is age 65 or older.

69. A
When a corporation files a registration with the SEC in an effort to sell shares to the public, the period of time between the filing of the registration statement and its effective date is referred to as the cooling-off period.

70. D

TRACE (Trade Reporting Compliance Engine) is the FINRA-developed vehicle that facilitates the mandatory reporting of over-the-counter secondary market transactions in eligible fixed income securities. All broker-dealers who are FINRA member firms have an obligation to report transactions in corporate bonds to TRACE under an SEC-approved set of rules.

71. A

A 403(b) plan may be adopted by an employer that is a state, agency of a state, nonprofit organization, public university, or private university.

72. C

Regarding IAR registration, all individual registrations are administered at the state level, regardless of whether the RIA firm is registered at the SEC or state level.

73. B

The NASAA (North American Securities Administrators Association) is the oldest international investor protection organization and is an association of state securities administrators who are charged with the responsibility to protect consumers who purchase securities or investment advice. Its membership consists of administrators from the territories, districts, and states of the U.S., Mexico, and Canada.

74. A

For the substantially equal periodic payment (SEPP) exception to apply for premature distributions from a retirement plan, payments must continue for 5 years or until the participant is age 59 ½, whichever is longer.

75. C

Mini-maxi underwriting is a type of best efforts underwriting that only becomes effective when a minimum amount of securities have been sold. Once the minimum requirement has been met, the underwriter may then sell securities up to a specified level under the terms of the offering.

PRACTICE EXAM 6

QUESTIONS

1. All but which of the following are characteristics of exchange-traded funds (ETFs)?

   A. They are traded on an exchange like individual securities.
   B. Their trades settle at the end of the trading day, similar to mutual funds.
   C. They have lower expenses than mutual funds.
   D. They are income tax efficient.

2. Monetary policy is carried out through all but which of the following methods?

   A. Open market operations
   B. Changing the discount rate
   C. Changing the reserve requirements
   D. Taxation

3. All but which of the following are correct regarding counter-cyclical stocks?

   A. They perform better during economic downturns.
   B. They are negatively correlated to the overall state of the economy.
   C. Examples of counter-cyclical stocks include airlines and hotels.
   D. They outperform during the contraction phase of the business cycle.

4. Which of the following is the market value of all the goods and services produced in one year by labor and property supplied by the citizens of a country, wherever they are located?

   A. GDP
   B. GNP
   C. NDP
   D. NNP

5. Which of the following is a notice made in the financial press that formally announces a particular transaction, such as an IPO or stock placement?

   A. Omitting prospectus
   B. Preliminary prospectus
   C. Red herring
   D. Tombstone ad

6. In which of the following accounts does a broker have the right to make significant investment decisions without permission from, or consultation with, the account owner?

   A. Custodian account
   B. Discretionary account
   C. Non-discretionary account
   D. Non-custodian account

7. Which of the following is a formal alternative to litigation in which two or more parties select a neutral third party to resolve a dispute? At the conclusion of this process, the final decision, referred to as the "award," is binding.

   A. Arbitration
   B. Mediation
   C. Remediation
   D. Revocation

8. Which of the following acts allowed for the establishment of the National Association of Securities Dealers (NASD) and the U.S. domestic over-the-counter markets in securities?

   A. Maloney Act of 1938
   B. Trust Indenture Act of 1939
   C. Investment Company Act of 1940
   D. Uniform Securities Act of 1956

9. John owns an investment yielding an after-tax return of 9.5%. If he is in the 15% tax bracket, what is the equivalent pre-tax return?

   A. 1.43%
   B. 8.08%
   C. 10.93%
   D. 11.18%

10. Which of the following preserves and promotes public confidence in the U.S. financial system by insuring deposits in banks by identifying, monitoring, and addressing risks to the deposit insurance funds; and by limiting the effect on the economy when a financial institution fails?

    A. FDIC
    B. NASD
    C. PBGC
    D. SIPC

11. An investment-grade bond is one that is rated _____ or higher by the Standard & Poor's bond rating service. A high-yield bond is rated _____ or lower by Standard & Poor's.

    A. BBB, BB
    B. BBB+, BB-
    C. BBB-, BB+
    D. BB, BBB

12. Which of the following is the electronic service that provides quotation information for stocks traded on the AMEX, NYSE, and other regional stock exchanges, and also includes issues traded by FINRA member firms in the third market?

    A. Alternative Trading System
    B. Consolidated Quotation System
    C. National Service Clearing Corporation
    D. Trade Reporting and Compliance Engine

13. Which of the following retirement plans would be most suitable to retain young employees?

    A. Cash balance plan
    B. Defined benefit plan
    C. Money purchase plan
    D. Target benefit plan

14. Which of the following refers to a computerized system used by the NYSE to display, record, and execute orders for securities?

    A. Automated quotation system
    B. Order management system
    C. Super display book system
    D. None of the above are correct.

15. The U.S. government conducts _____ policy through government spending and taxation.

    A. fiscal
    B. fiscal and monetary
    C. open market
    D. monetary

16. Which of the following refers to direct institution-to-institution trading, usually done in blocks, without using the service of broker-dealers?

    A. First market
    B. Second market
    C. Third market
    D. Fourth market

17. Contractionary policy is characterized by which of the following?

    A. Increasing government borrowing
    B. Increasing public spending
    C. Increasing taxes
    D. All of the above are correct.

18. Which of the following is a group of investment banks that work together to sell new security offerings to investors?

    A. Registration syndicate
    B. Subscription syndicate
    C. Underwriting syndicate
    D. None of the above are correct.

19. According to the Uniform Securities Act, which of the following are classified as securities?

    A. Collectibles
    B. Fixed annuities
    C. Warrants
    D. Whole life insurance policies

20. When calculating gross domestic product (GDP), all but which of the following variables are paired with the correct description?

    A. C = Personal consumption
    B. I = Issuance of government bonds
    C. G = Government spending
    D. E = Net exports

21. The "cooling-off period," which transpires between the filing of a new issue's prospectus and the actual offering of the issue, must be a minimum of how many days?

    A. 7 days
    B. 10 days
    C. 20 days
    D. 30 days

22. Which of the following is a short-term obligation that is issued for temporary financing needs by a municipality?

    A. Bond anticipation note
    B. Guaranteed investment contract
    C. Tax anticipation note
    D. Unit investment trust

23. Kappa Inc., a growing IT company based in California, plans to launch its IPO this year. The IPO will be regulated by which of the following laws?

    A. Securities Act of 1933
    B. Securities Act of 1934
    C. Investment Company Act of 1940
    D. SIPC of 1970

24. _____ risk cannot be eliminated through diversification because it affects the entire market. _____ risk may be diversified away or avoided by not investing in securities that exhibit the risk.

    A. Non-systematic, Unsystematic
    B. Unsystematic, Systematic
    C. Systematic, Unsystematic
    D. Total, Systematic

25. Treasury notes, Treasury bonds, and TIPS, whose interest and principal portions have been separated so they may be sold individually, are referred to as which of the following?

    A. Treasury GICs
    B. Treasury CMOs
    C. Treasury STRIPS
    D. Treasury UITs

26. Which of the following is the initial registration form for new securities required by the SEC for U.S.-based public companies?

    A. Form F-1
    B. Form S-1
    C. Form T-1
    D. Form U-1

For questions 27 – 29, match the cost recovery term with the description that follows. Use only one answer per blank. Answers may be used more than once or not at all.

    A. Amortization
    B. Depreciation
    C. Depletion

27. ___ The process by which the tax basis of natural resources is recovered.

28. ___ The process by which the tax basis of intangible assets is recovered.

29. ___ The process by which the tax basis of tangible assets is recovered.

30. Which of the following describes a strategy used to minimize the interest rate risk of bond investments by adjusting the portfolio duration to match the investment time horizon?

    A. Bond hedging
    B. Bond immunization
    C. Bond laddering
    D. Bond spread

31. Which of the following is a broker that processes a buy or sell order on behalf of a client?

    A. Carrying broker
    B. Clearing broker
    C. Executing broker
    D. Introducing broker

32. Which of the following is a measure of the timing of cash flows (i.e., the interest payments and the principal repayment) to be received from a fixed income security? It's used to assess price volatility for changes in interest rates and the reinvestment risk associated with a portfolio.

    A. Convexity
    B. Duration
    C. Term
    D. Yield

33. Which of the following options will put an investor at the greatest risk?

    A. Buying a put while not owning the stock.
    B. Buying a put while owning the stock.
    C. Selling a stock short while not owning the stock.
    D. Selling a stock short while owning the stock.

34. Which of the following measures the level of trading activity within a mutual fund?

    A. Capitalization rate
    B. Expense rate
    C. Price/earnings rate
    D. Turnover rate

35. Which of the following are permitted distribution options from a qualified retirement plan?

    (1) Lump sum distribution
    (2) Direct trustee-to-trustee transfer
    (3) Payment in the form of an annuity or other periodic payment option
    (4) Rollover of funds from one qualified retirement plan to another

    A. (1) and (3) only
    B. (1), (2), and (4) only
    C. (2), (3), and (4) only
    D. All of the above are correct.

36. Which of the following is correct regarding convertible bonds?

A. They typically offer lower coupon rates than non-convertible bonds issued for the same term by the same issuer.
B. They typically offer higher coupon rates than non-convertible bonds issued for the same term by the same issuer.
C. They typically offer the same coupon rates as non-convertible bonds issued for the same term by the same issuer.
D. They are zero-coupon bonds issued at a discount to par.

For questions 37 – 41, match each security description with the term that follows. Use only one answer per blank. Answers may be used more than once or not at all.

A. Freely traded in the secondary markets; yield and term are determined at the time of purchase.
B. Pay a fixed rate of interest every six months until maturity; issued in terms of ten years or more.
C. Can be redeemed at any time without penalty; objective is to earn interest for shareholders.
D. Unsecured promissory note issued by corporations with a fixed maturity of up to 270 days.
E. Intended to be held until maturity, but can be redeemed prior to maturity for a penalty.
F. Dividends are declared in local currencies and paid in U.S. dollars.

37. ___ Money market funds

38. ___ Certificate of deposit

39. ___ Commercial paper

40. ___ Treasury bonds

41. ___ American Depository Receipts

42. All but which of the following are types of REITs?

A. Equity REIT
B. Hybrid REIT
C. Mortgage REIT
D. All of the above are correct.

43. A hedge fund is a _____ offered fund of securities for high-net worth investors. The hedge fund manager is generally paid a _____ fee.

A. privately, flat
B. privately, performance
C. publicly, flat
D. publicly, performance

44. Which of the following is/are correct regarding beta?

(1) It is used to measure the amount of unsystematic risk in an investor's portfolio.
(2) A portfolio's beta can be positive or equal to zero, but cannot be negative.

A. (1) only
B. (2) only
C. Both (1) and (2) are correct.
D. Neither (1) or (2) are correct.

45. All but which of the following are correct regarding subordinated debentures?

A. In the event of liquidation, they are prioritized lower than other classes of debt.
B. This class of debt carries less risk, and therefore pays lower interest, than other classes.
C. They are unsecured loans which have no collateral.
D. They are a type of junior debt.

46. Which of the following is an order to purchase a security at or below a specified price?

A. Buy stop order
B. Buy market order
C. Buy limit order
D. None of the above are correct.

47. All but which of the following are correct regarding Treasury bills?

A. They have maturities of one year or less.
B. They are sold in minimum denominations of $500.
C. They are considered to be risk free of default.
D. They are sold at a discount to par.

48. Which of the following is a type of preferred stock in which the issuer has the right to redeem the stock at a preset price after a predetermined date?

A. Callable preferred stock
B. Common preferred stock
C. Diluted preferred stock
D. Subordinate preferred stock

49. Inflation is measured by which of the following?

A. CPI
B. GNI
C. GNP
D. NNI

50. Which of the following is a value-weighted index measuring the overall performance of the U.S. stock market?

    A. Dow Jones Industrial Average
    B. EAFE Index
    C. Russell 2000
    D. Wilshire 5000

51. To establish a Coverdell Education Savings Account (ESA), the beneficiary must be under age _____ unless the individual is designated as a special needs beneficiary.

    A. 14
    B. 18
    C. 21
    D. 30

52. An investor purchased a 5-year bond that pays a 3.5% semiannual coupon payment. The bond is priced at $97 per $100 of par value. What is the bond's current yield?

    A. 3.50%
    B. 3.61%
    C. 7.22%
    D. 7.65%

53. Which of the following are permitted investments in a 403(b) plan?

    (1) Mutual funds
    (2) Bond funds
    (3) Treasury bills
    (4) Life insurance that is incidental to an annuity contract

    A. (1) and (4) only
    B. (2) and (3) only
    C. (1), (2), and (4) only
    D. All of the above are correct.

54. Which of the following is the prohibited practice of entering into an equity trade to capitalize on advance, nonpublic knowledge of a large pending transaction that will influence the price of the underlying security?

    A. Capping
    B. Front running
    C. Painting the tape
    D. Pegging

55. An investment adviser that has custody of client assets must file an audited balance sheet with the SEC within how many days of the investment adviser's fiscal year end?

   A. 30 days
   B. 60 days
   C. 90 days
   D. 120 days

56. Which of the following is a characteristic of a debenture bond?

   A. Debenture bonds are secured bonds.
   B. Debenture bondholders have the same rights as general creditors.
   C. To account for the lower default risk, debenture bonds will have lower yields to maturity than secured bonds issued for the same term by the same issuer.
   D. All of the above are correct.

57. Which of the following is the ethical barrier that is required between different divisions of a financial institution to avoid conflicts of interest?

   A. Checks and balance system
   B. Chinese wall
   C. Ethical wall
   D. Moral barrier

58. Which of the following is correct regarding Electronic Communication Networks (ECNs)?

   A. All registered investment advisers are permitted to become ECN subscribers.
   B. ECNs are not permitted to become members of FINRA.
   C. An execution occurs when the price of a buy order and the price of a sell order intersect on the ECN.
   D. All of the above are correct.

59. Dealers report municipal securities transaction data through which of the following?

   A. ACATS
   B. NSCC
   C. OATS
   D. RTRS

60. According to the T+2 settlement cycle, shares of stock that are sold on Monday will settle on:

   A. Tuesday.
   B. Wednesday.
   C. Thursday.
   D. Friday.

61. Which of the following acts established a non-profit membership corporation that oversees the liquidation of member broker-dealers that close when the broker-dealer is bankrupt or in financial trouble, and customer assets are missing?

   A. Securities Investor Protection Corporation Act of 1970
   B. Securities Act Amendments of 1975
   C. Uniform Prudent Investors Act of 1994
   D. National Securities Market Improvement Act of 1996

The following information relates to questions 62 – 63.

Beta Corporation, a broker-dealer, would like to withdraw their state registration.

62. Which of the following forms must Beta Corporation submit to withdraw registration?

   A. Form ADV-W
   B. Form BDW
   C. Form BR
   D. Form W

63. The withdrawal will become effective _____ following the SEC's receipt of the form, unless the division notifies Beta Corporation otherwise.

   A. 30 days
   B. 60 days
   C. 90 days
   D. 120 days

64. Which of the following is the result of persistent high inflation combined with high unemployment and a slowing demand for goods and services?

   A. Deflation
   B. Inflation
   C. Reflation
   D. Stagflation

65. Which of the following is a statement on a stock certificate noting restrictions on the transfer of the stock? It contains language informing the holder of the restrictions on the sale or transfer of the unregistered security.

   A. Declaration
   B. Legend
   C. Medallion
   D. Warranty

66. Which of the following documents is sent to shareholders informing them of when and where a shareholders' meeting is taking place? It also details the matters to be voted on during the meeting.

    A. Offering circular
    B. Program disclosure
    C. Prospectus
    D. Proxy statement

67. Banks and credit unions must file a Suspicious Activity Report if a transaction involves or aggregates at least _____ in funds or other assets, and the institution knows, suspects, or has reason to suspect that the transaction is designed to evade the requirements of the Bank Secrecy Act.

    A. $5,000
    B. $10,000
    C. $25,000
    D. $100,000

68. All but which of the following are correct regarding FinCEN?

    A. Its mission is to provide a network to support the detection, investigation, and prosecution of domestic and international money laundering and other financial crimes.
    B. It uses counter-money laundering laws, such as the Bank Secrecy Act, to require reporting and recordkeeping by banks and other financial institutions.
    C. It administers and enforces economic and trade sanctions against threats to the national security, foreign policy, or economy of the United States.
    D. It provides intelligence and analytical support to law enforcement and works to maximize information sharing among law enforcement agencies.

69. Which of the following are among the goals of the Federal Reserve?

    A. To achieve full employment.
    B. To minimize systematic risk.
    C. To stabilize prices.
    D. All of the above are correct.

70. Which of the following is correct regarding the taxation of Treasury STRIPS?

    A. Tax must be paid on accrued interest each year even though no interest is received by the investor.
    B. Tax is not paid on accrued interest each year because no interest is received by the investor.
    C. Tax must be paid at maturity only.
    D. Treasury STRIPS are not taxed.

71. Higher inflation = _____ interest rates = _____ bond values

    A. higher, higher
    B. higher, lower
    C. lower, higher
    D. lower, lower

72. In a short call, the maximum gain is _____ and the maximum loss is _____.

    A. unlimited, the premium paid
    B. the premium paid, unlimited
    C. unlimited, unlimited
    D. limited, limited

73. In which of the following qualified retirement plans are the employees responsible for the investment risk?

    (1) Money purchase plans
    (2) Target benefit plans
    (3) Defined benefit plans
    (4) Cash balance plans

    A. (1) and (3) only
    B. (1) and (2) only
    C. (2) and (3) only
    D. (3) and (4) only

74. Which of the following holds deposit securities owned by broker-dealers, arranges the receipt and delivery of securities between users by means of debiting and crediting their respective accounts, and arranges for payment of monies between users in the settlement of transactions?

    A. DTC
    B. NBBO
    C. OATS
    D. RTRS

75. Which of the following is a settlement method in which the transfer of securities and associated payment occurs simultaneously? It ensures that the final transfer of a security occurs only if the final transfer of the associated payment also occurs.

    A. Delivery vs. Free
    B. Delivery vs. Payment
    C. Delivery vs. Receipt
    D. Delivery vs. Settlement

ANSWER KEY

1. B
Exchange-traded funds (ETFs) may be bought or sold throughout the trading day like individual securities. They have lower expenses than mutual funds and are income tax efficient.

2. D
Monetary policy is carried out through open market operations, changing the discount rate, and changing the reserve requirements.

3. C
Counter-cyclical stocks perform better during economic downturns because they are negatively correlated to the overall state of the economy. They outperform during the contraction phase of the business cycle. Examples of counter-cyclical stocks include debt collectors, discount retailers, and alcoholic beverage manufacturers.

4. B
GNP (gross national product) is the market value of all the goods and services produced in one year by labor and property supplied by the citizens of a country, wherever they are located.

5. D
A tombstone ad is a notice made in the financial press that formally announces a particular transaction, such as an IPO or stock placement.

6. B
In a discretionary account, a broker has the right to make significant investment decisions without permission from, or consultation with, the account owner.

7. A
Arbitration is a formal alternative to litigation in which two or more parties select a neutral third party to resolve a dispute. At the conclusion of this process, the final decision, referred to as the "award," is binding.

8. A
The Maloney Act of 1938 allowed for the establishment of the National Association of Securities Dealers (NASD) and the U.S. domestic over-the-counter markets in securities.

9. D
Pre-tax return = $0.095 \div (1 - 0.15) = 0.1118 = 11.18\%$

10. A
The FDIC preserves and promotes public confidence in the U.S. financial system by insuring deposits in banks by identifying, monitoring, and addressing risks to the deposit insurance funds; and by limiting the effect on the economy when a financial institution fails.

11. C
An investment-grade bond is one that is rated BBB- or higher by the Standard & Poor's bond rating service. A high-yield bond is rated BB+ or lower by Standard & Poor's.

12. B
The Consolidated Quotation System (CQS) is the electronic service that provides quotation information for stocks traded on the AMEX, NYSE, and other regional stock exchanges, and also includes issues traded by FINRA member firms in the third market.

13. C
The cash balance plan, defined benefit plan, and target benefit plan all favor older employees. The money purchase plan favors younger employees.

14. C
The super display book system is a computerized system used by the NYSE to display, record, and execute orders for securities.

15. A
The U.S. government conducts fiscal policy through government spending and taxation.

16. D
The fourth market refers to direct institution-to-institution trading, usually done in blocks, without using the service of broker-dealers.

17. C
Contractionary policy is characterized by increasing taxes, decreasing government borrowing, and decreasing public spending.

18. C
An underwriting syndicate is a group of investment banks that work together to sell new security offerings to investors.

19. C
According to the Uniform Securities Act, warrants are classified as securities. Collectibles, fixed annuities, and whole life insurance policies are not classified as securities.

20. B
Gross Domestic Product (GDP) $= C + I + G + E$
C = Personal consumption
I = Gross private domestic investment
G = Government spending
E = Net exports

21. C
The "cooling-off period," which transpires between the filing of a new issue's prospectus and the actual offering of the issue, must be a minimum of 20 days.

22. A
A bond anticipation note (BAN) is a short-term obligation that is issued for temporary financing needs by a municipality.

23. A
The Securities Act of 1933 regulates new securities, including IPOs.

24. C

Systematic risk cannot be eliminated through diversification because it affects the entire market. Unsystematic risk may be diversified away or avoided by not investing in securities that exhibit the risk.

25. C

Treasury notes, Treasury bonds, and TIPS, whose interest and principal portions have been separated so they may be sold individually, are referred to as Treasury STRIPS.

26. B

Form S-1 is the initial registration form for new securities required by the SEC for U.S.-based public companies.

27. C

Depletion is the process by which the tax basis of natural resources is recovered.

28. A

Amortization is the process by which the tax basis of intangible assets is recovered.

29. B

Depreciation is the process by which the tax basis of tangible assets is recovered.

30. B

Bond immunization is an investment strategy used to minimize the interest rate risk of bond investments by adjusting the portfolio duration to match the investment time horizon.

31. C

An executing broker processes a buy or sell order on behalf of a client.

32. B

Duration is a measure of the timing of cash flows (i.e., the interest payments and the principal repayment) to be received from a fixed income security. It's used to assess price volatility for changes in interest rates and the reinvestment risk associated with a portfolio.

33. C

Selling a stock short without already owning the stock would put an investor at the greatest risk. If the stock increases in value, the investor would have to repurchase the stock on the open market. However, if the investor already owned the stock, she would benefit from the shares appreciating in value.

34. D

The turnover rate measures the level of trading activity within a mutual fund.

35. D

The permitted distribution options from a qualified retirement plan are lump sum distribution, direct trustee-to-trustee transfer, payment in the form of an annuity or other periodic payment option, and rollover of funds from one qualified retirement plan to another.

36. A
Because of their flexibility, convertible bonds typically offer lower coupon rates than non-convertible bonds issued for the same term by the same issuer.

37. C
Money market funds can be redeemed at any time without penalty. Their objective is to earn interest for shareholders.

38. E
A certificate of deposit is intended to be held until maturity, but can be redeemed prior to maturity for a penalty.

39. D
Commercial paper is an unsecured promissory note issued by a corporation with a fixed maturity of up to 270 days.

40. B
Treasury bonds pay a fixed rate of interest every six months until maturity. They are issued in terms of ten years or more.

41. F
American Depository Receipt dividends are declared in local currencies and paid in U.S. dollars.

42. D
The three main types of REITs are equity REITs, mortgage REITs, and hybrid REITs.

43. B
A hedge fund is a privately offered fund of securities for high-net worth investors. The hedge fund manager is generally paid a performance fee.

44. D
Beta is used to measure the amount of systematic risk in an investor's portfolio. A portfolio's beta can be positive, negative, or equal to zero.

45. B
In the event of liquidation, subordinated debentures are prioritized lower than other classes of debt. They are unsecured loans which have no collateral, and they are a type of junior debt. Subordinated debentures carry higher risk, but also pays higher interest, than other classes.

46. C
A buy limit order is an order to purchase a security at or below a specified price.

47. B
Treasury bills are sold at a discount to par and have maturities of one year or less. They are considered to be risk free of default and are sold in minimum denominations of $1,000.

48. A

Callable preferred stock is a type of preferred stock in which the issuer has the right to redeem the stock at a preset price after a predetermined date.

49. A

Inflation is measured by the CPI (Consumer Price Index).

50. D

The Wilshire 5000 is a value-weighted index measuring the overall performance of the U.S. stock market.

51. B

To establish a Coverdell Education Savings Account (ESA), the beneficiary must be under age 18 unless the individual is designated as a special needs beneficiary.

52. B

Current yield = Sum of coupon payments ÷ Market price
Current yield = ($100 × 0.035) ÷ $97 = 0.0361 = 3.61%

53. C

Mutual funds, bonds funds, and life insurance that is incidental to an annuity contract are permitted investments in a 403(b) plan.

54. B

Front running is the prohibited practice of entering into an equity trade to capitalize on advance, nonpublic knowledge of a large pending transaction that will influence the price of the underlying security.

55. C

An investment adviser that has custody of client assets must file an audited balance sheet with the SEC within 90 days of the investment adviser's fiscal year end.

56. B

Debenture bonds are unsecured bonds, and debenture bondholders have the same rights as general creditors. To account for the higher default risk, debenture bonds will have higher yields to maturities than secured bonds issued for the same term by the same issuer.

57. B

A Chinese wall is the ethical barrier that is required between different divisions of a financial institution to avoid conflicts of interest.

58. C

ECNs are members of FINRA, and, typically, only broker-dealers and certain institutional traders are permitted to become ECN subscribers. An execution occurs when the price of a buy order and the price of a sell order intersect on the ECN.

59. D

Dealers report municipal securities transaction data through the RTRS (Real-Time Transaction Reporting System).

60. B

According to the T+2 settlement cycle, shares of stock that are sold on Monday will settle on Wednesday.

61. A

The Securities Investor Protection Corporation Act of 1970 established a non-profit membership corporation that oversees the liquidation of member broker-dealers that close when the broker-dealer is bankrupt or in financial trouble, and customer assets are missing.

62. B

Beta Corporation must submit Form BDW to withdraw their state registration.

63. A

The withdrawal will become effective 30 days following the SEC's receipt of the form, unless the division notifies Beta Corporation otherwise.

64. D

Stagflation is the result of persistent high inflation combined with high unemployment and a slowing demand for goods and services.

65. B

A legend is a statement on a stock certificate noting restrictions on the transfer of the stock. It contains language informing the holder of the restrictions on the sale or transfer of the unregistered security.

66. D

A proxy statement is sent to shareholders informing them of when and where a shareholders' meeting is taking place. It also details the matters to be voted on during the meeting.

67. A

Banks and credit unions must file a Suspicious Activity Report if a transaction involves or aggregates at least $5,000 in funds or other assets, and the institution knows, suspects, or has reason to suspect that the transaction is designed to evade the requirements of the Bank Secrecy Act.

68. C

FinCEN's mission is to provide a network to support the detection, investigation, and prosecution of domestic and international money laundering and other financial crimes. It uses counter-money laundering laws, such as the Bank Secrecy Act, to require reporting and recordkeeping by banks and other financial institutions, and it provides intelligence and analytical support to law enforcement and works to maximize information sharing among law enforcement agencies. (The OFAC, not FinCEN, administers and enforces economic and trade sanctions against threats to the national security, foreign policy, or economy of the United States.)

69. D

The goals of the Federal Reserve are to achieve full employment, minimize systematic risk, and stabilize prices.

70. A
For Treasury STRIPS, tax must be paid on accrued interest each year even though no interest is received by the investor.

71. B
Higher inflation = higher interest rates = lower bond values

72. B
In a short call, the maximum gain is the premium paid and the maximum loss is unlimited.

73. B
The employee assumes the investment risk in a defined contribution plan. Money purchase plans and target benefit plans are types of defined contribution plans.

74. A
The DTC (Depository Trust Company) holds deposit securities owned by broker-dealers, arranges the receipt and delivery of securities between users by means of debiting and crediting their respective accounts, and arranges for payment of monies between users in the settlement of transactions.

75. B
Delivery vs. Payment (DVP) is a settlement method in which the transfer of securities and associated payment occurs simultaneously. It ensures that the final transfer of a security occurs only if the final transfer of the associated payment also occurs.

PRACTICE EXAM 7

QUESTIONS

1. All but which of the following information is commonly found in a mutual fund prospectus?

   A. Fees and expenses
   B. Investment objectives
   C. Principal risks of investing in the fund
   D. All of the above are correct.

2. Delta Corporation has retained earnings of $100,000, and they plan to use the funds to either invest in common stock or hire two new employees. Assuming these are mutually exclusive events, which of the following refers to the potential benefit that is lost by choosing one of these options over the other?

   A. Budget constraint
   B. Opportunity cost
   C. Production-possibility frontier
   D. Prospect theory

3. With certain exceptions, which of the following acts requires that firms or sole practitioners compensated for advising others about securities investments must register with the SEC and conform to regulations designed to protect investors?

   A. Securities Act of 1933
   B. Securities Exchange Act of 1934
   C. Investment Advisers Act of 1940
   D. Investment Company Act of 1940

4. Which of the following are among the economic goals of the Federal Reserve and the U.S. Treasury?

   (1) Full employment
   (2) Stable prices
   (3) Economic growth
   (4) Decrease government spending

   A. (1) and (4) only
   B. (3) and (4) only
   C. (1), (2), and (3) only
   D. All of the above are correct.

5. All but which of the following is another name for an income statement?

   A. Statement of financial performance
   B. Statement of financial position
   C. Statement of operations
   D. Statement of profit or loss

6. Which of the following is/are correct regarding the capital structure of closed-end mutual funds?

   (1) A closed-end mutual fund has a fixed number of shares that, after original issue, trade on the secondary market.
   (2) The price an investor pays when buying shares of a closed-end mutual fund is based on supply and demand.

   A. (1) only
   B. (2) only
   C. Both (1) and (2) are correct.
   D. Neither (1) or (2) are correct.

7. All but which of the following are potential benefits of a bond swap?

   A. It can reduce an investor's tax liability.
   B. It can provide a higher rate of return.
   C. It can provide investment diversification.
   D. All of the above are correct.

8. A stock with a beta of –1.5 and a standard deviation of 10.1 will change in which of the following ways if the stock market increases 8%?

   A. Increase by 4%
   B. Increase by 8%
   C. Decrease by 10%
   D. Decrease by 12%

9. Which of the following is a weighted index of prices measured at the wholesale level?

   A. CPI
   B. GNP
   C. NNI
   D. PPI

10. Which of the following is/are correct regarding cyclical stocks?

   (1) When the economy is growing, demand usually strengthens and cyclical companies are able to make large profits.
   (2) When the economy is declining, cyclical companies are hurt by decreases in demand and are less profitable.

   A. (1) only
   B. (2) only
   C. Both (1) and (2) are correct.
   D. Neither (1) or (2) are correct.

11. Which of the following refers to the cash held in an investor's margin account at a broker-dealer that can be withdrawn at any time? It may include interest, dividends, and coupon payments.

    A. Average daily balance
    B. Free credit balance
    C. Liquidation margin
    D. Margin balance

12. The Dow Jones Utility Average is an index comprised of _____ utility stocks, and the Dow Jones Transportation Average is an index comprised of _____ transportation stocks.

    A. 10, 30
    B. 15, 20
    C. 20, 50
    D. 30, 50

13. Which of the following is a group of underwriters who agree to purchase the shares of an IPO from an issuer and then sell the shares to investors?

    A. Registered investment advisers
    B. Regulated investment company
    C. Solicitors
    D. Syndicate

14. Which of the following is correct regarding TIPS?

    A. Investors are paid either the adjusted principal amount at maturity, or the original principal amount, whichever is greater.
    B. They pay interest annually.
    C. The payments increase with inflation but never decrease.
    D. They have a final maturity up to 10 years from the date of issue.

15. Which of the following is also referred to as a "red herring?"

    A. Omitting prospectus
    B. Preliminary prospectus
    C. Shelf registration
    D. Tombstone ad

16. In a long call, the maximum gain is _____ and the maximum loss is _____.

    A. limited, unlimited
    B. the premium paid, unlimited
    C. unlimited, the premium paid
    D. unlimited, unlimited

17. Which of the following is a computerized subscriber service that serves as a vehicle for the fourth market by permitting subscribers to display bids and offers and execute trades electronically?

A. ECN
B. EMMA
C. Instinet
D. NSCC

18. An indenture agreement describes the terms and conditions of a bond, including which of the following?

A. Call provisions
B. Description of collateral
C. How coupon payments are determined
D. All of the above are correct.

19. All but which of the following are correct regarding FINRA's emergency preparedness rule?

A. A firm must disclose to its customers how its business continuity plan addresses the possibility of a significant business disruption and how the firm plans to respond to events of varying scope.
B. A firm's business continuity plan must be made available promptly to FINRA staff if requested.
C. A firm's business continuity plan must be reasonably designed so the firm can meet its existing obligations to customers.
D. A firm's business continuity plan may be kept confidential from clients.

For questions 20 – 25, match the type of risk with the description that follows. Use only one answer per blank. Answers may be used more than once or not at all.

A. Systematic risk
B. Unsystematic risk

20. ___ Purchasing power risk

21. ___ Business risk

22. ___ Market risk

23. ___ Financial risk

24. ___ Interest rate risk

25. ___ Exchange rate risk

26. Which of the following is the penalty for a premature distribution from a qualified plan, 403(b) plan, IRA, or SEP?

   A. 5%
   B. 10%
   C. 15%
   D. Ordinary income tax rates

27. Which of the following acts, also known as the Currency and Foreign Transactions Reporting Act, requires financial institutions to assist U.S. government agencies in detecting and preventing money laundering?

   A. Bank Secrecy Act of 1970
   B. Insider Trading and Securities Fraud Enforcement Act of 1988
   C. National Securities Market Improvement Act of 1996
   D. Sarbanes-Oxley Act of 2002

28. An investment-grade bond is one that is rated _____ or higher by Moody's. A high-yield bond is rated _____ or lower by Moody's.

   A. Ba, Baa
   B. Baa, Ba
   C. Baa3, Ba1
   D. Baa+, Ba-

29. Which of the following is the formula to calculate a mutual fund's turnover rate?

   A. Turnover rate = Gross proceeds from sale of securities ÷ NAV
   B. Turnover rate = Gross proceeds from sale of securities – NAV
   C. Turnover rate = Gross proceeds from sale of securities + NAV
   D. Turnover rate = NAV ÷ Gross proceeds from sale of securities

30. All but which of the following are correct regarding breakpoints?

   A. If a mutual fund charges a front-end sales load of 5% for purchases of less than $50,000, and 4% for purchases between $50,000 and $99,999, the level at which the discount becomes available is known as the breakpoint.
   B. A right of accumulation (ROA) typically provides a discount to current mutual fund purchases by combining both current and previous fund transactions to reach a breakpoint.
   C. A letter of intent (LOI) is a statement provided by an investor that expresses the intent to invest an amount over the breakpoint within a given period of time specified by the fund.
   D. In the case of ROAs and LOIs, investors are generally not permitted to credit mutual fund transactions in different mutual fund classes toward breakpoint discounts.

31. Which of the following is a manipulative trading activity that is designed to prevent the price of a security from falling?

    A. Capping
    B. Front running
    C. Painting the tape
    D. Pegging

32. All but which of the following are correct regarding a convertible bond?

    A. It is a type of corporate bond that may be converted into common stock of the issuing corporation.
    B. It may be converted at the bondholder's discretion.
    C. It allows an investor to share in the growth of the corporation only if the bond is converted into common stock.
    D. It is a zero-coupon bond issued at a discount to par.

33. The Federal Trade Commission implemented which of the following rules that requires broker-dealers and other financial institutions to create a written identity theft prevention program designed to detect the warning signs of identity theft in their day-to-day operations?

    A. CTR Rule
    B. Red Flags Rule
    C. SRO Rule
    D. Whistleblower Rule

34. What is the taxable equivalent yield of a municipal bond that has a tax-free yield of 6%? Assume the investor is in the 28% tax bracket.

    A. 4.69%
    B. 7.68%
    C. 8.33%
    D. 21.43%

35. All but which of the following are correct regarding a futures contract?

    A. It is an agreement to buy or sell a specific quantity of a commodity or financial currency at a predetermined price on a specific future date.
    B. The holder of a futures contract cannot purchase an offsetting contract that cancels the original position, rather than receiving delivery of the commodity.
    C. Commodities such as grains, metals, and natural gas do not have tradable futures contracts.
    D. All of the above are correct.

36. Which of the following is a 9-digit alphanumeric code assigned to each maturity of a municipal security issue?

    A. CUSIP
    B. MPID
    C. Serial number
    D. Ticker symbol

37. Which of the following allow individuals with disabilities and their families to save money for disability-related expenses of the account's designated beneficiary in a tax-advantaged way?

    A. ABLE accounts
    B. ESOP accounts
    C. HOPE accounts
    D. SSI accounts

38. A research analyst provides the following economic information for Country X:

Category	Amount ($ billions)
Consumption	11.4
Government spending	3.3
Capital consumption allowance	5.0
Gross private domestic investment	6.2
Imports	2.9
Exports	1.8

What is the gross domestic product (GDP) of Country X?

    A. $17.9 billion
    B. $18.6 billion
    C. $19.8 billion
    D. $24.8 billion

39. Which of the following are correct regarding a bond's yield to maturity (YTM)?

    (1) The YTM assumes that coupon payments are reinvested at the YTM rate of return for the life of the bond.
    (2) When the market rate of interest for the same term and risk is higher than the coupon rate, a discount will be priced into the bond.
    (3) Bonds that are riskier will have lower yields to maturity.
    (4) The YTM is the internal rate of return for cash flow associated with a bond, including the purchase price, coupon payments, and maturity value.

    A. (1) and (2) only
    B. (3) and (4) only
    C. (1), (2), and (4) only
    D. (1), (3), and (4) only

40. Which of the following yield curves results from short-term debt instruments having a lower yield than long-term debt instruments of the same credit quality?

    A. Flat yield curve
    B. Inverted yield curve
    C. Normal yield curve
    D. Steep yield curve

For questions 41 – 43, match the dividend date with the description that follows. Use only one answer per blank. Answers may be used more than once or not at all.

    A. Date of declaration
    B. Ex-dividend date
    C. Date of record
    D. Date of payment

41. ___ The date that the board of directors approves and decides that a dividend will be paid.

42. ___ The date that it is determined who owns stock in the company and is entitled to receive a dividend.

43. ___ The date that the market price of the stock adjusts for the dividend.

44. Carrie believes the share price of Zeta stock will decrease in the short term. She has decided to sell short 500 shares at the current market price of $89. If the initial margin requirement is 35%, what amount must Carrie contribute as margin?

    A. $15,575
    B. $17,250
    C. $19,925
    D. $21,485

45. Which of the following is correct regarding the relationship between a bond's coupon and its duration?

    A. Higher coupon = Lower duration = Lower interest rate risk
    B. Higher coupon = Higher duration = Higher interest rate risk
    C. Higher coupon = Lower duration = Higher interest rate risk
    D. Higher coupon = Higher duration = Lower interest rate risk

46. The initial margin percentage is currently _____ as established by Regulation T of the Federal Reserve Board.

    A. 25%
    B. 30%
    C. 50%
    D. 75%

47. Which of the following are among the exemptions from the 10% early withdrawal penalty from an IRA?

(1) Higher education costs for the account owner's child.
(2) Hardship withdrawals.
(3) A first-time home purchase up to $10,000.
(4) Separation from employment service at age 55 or older.
(5) A loan for medical expenses.

A. (1) and (3) only
B. (2) and (4) only
C. (3) and (5) only
D. (1), (3), and (4) only

48. Which of the following is a note issued in anticipation of future tax receipts, such as receipts of ad valorem taxes that are due and payable at a set time of year?

A. BAN
B. RAN
C. TAN
D. TRAN

For questions 49 – 53, match the term with the description that follows. Use only one answer per blank. Answers may be used more than once or not at all.

A. Call loan rate
B. Discount rate
C. Fed funds rate
D. LIBOR
E. Prime rate

49. ___ The minimum interest rate set by the Federal Reserve for lending to other banks.

50. ___ The interest rate at which depository institutions (banks and credit unions) lend reserve balances to other depository institutions overnight, on a collateralized basis.

51. ___ The short-term interest rate charged by banks on loans extended to broker-dealers, who then use the funds to make margin loans on behalf of customers.

52. ___ The interest rate that banks charge their most credit-worthy customers, typically large corporations.

53. ___ The benchmark rate that international banks charge each other for short-term loans.

54. Which of the following is the minimum age requirement to use the substantially equal period payment (SEPP) exception to the 10% premature distribution penalty from an IRA?

   A. Age 21
   B. Age 59 ½
   C. Age 65
   D. There is no minimum age requirement.

55. Which of the following acts provides the tools required to intercept and obstruct terrorism? Title III of this act is intended to facilitate the prevention, detection, and prosecution of international money laundering and the financing of terrorism.

   A. Insider Trading and Securities Fraud Enforcement Act of 1988
   B. Patriot Act of 2001
   C. Sarbanes-Oxley Act of 2002
   D. Dodd-Frank Wall Street Reform and Consumer Protection Act of 2010

56. Which of the following is required for an individual to open a health savings account (HSA)?

   A. The individual must have a high-deductible health plan (HDHP).
   B. The individual must have a low-deductible health plan (LDHP).
   C. The individual must have a flexible spending account (FSA).
   D. None of the above are required to open a health savings account.

57. Which of the following is the maximum prison sentence for an insider trading violation?

   A. 10 years
   B. 20 years
   C. 30 years
   D. 40 years

58. Which of the following investment strategies are profitable in a rising stock market?

   (1) Buying a call
   (2) Buying a put
   (3) Selling a put
   (4) Selling a call

   A. (1) and (3) only
   B. (1) and (4) only
   C. (2) and (3) only
   D. (2) and (4) only

59. Which of the following is a subscription service operated by NASDAQ that automates trades between order entry and market maker firms that have established trading relationships with each other?

A. ACES
B. DTCC
C. OATS
D. RTRS

60. Which of the following administers and enforces economic and trade sanctions based on U.S. foreign policy and national security goals against targeted foreign countries and terrorist threats to the national security, foreign policy, or economy of the United States?

A. Department of Foreign Affairs
B. Department of Homeland Security
C. Office of Foreign Assets Control
D. Office of Securities Fraud Enforcement

61. According to FINRA guidelines, a broker or dealer shall maintain net capital of not less than _____ if it acts as a broker or dealer with respect to the purchase, sale, and redemption of redeemable shares of registered investment companies.

A. $10,000
B. $25,000
C. $50,000
D. $100,000

62. Which of the following is/are correct regarding durable powers of attorney?

(1) A durable power of attorney survives the death of the principal.
(2) A durable power of attorney survives disability of both the principal and the agent.

A. (1) only
B. (2) only
C. Both (1) and (2) are correct.
D. Neither (1) or (2) are correct.

63. Which of the following describes the characteristics and risks of standardized options to be traded in a particular market, and is mandated by the Securities Exchange Act of 1934?

A. Derivatives offering circular
B. Options disclosure document
C. Options proxy agreement
D. Options registration statement

64. According to the Uniform Securities Act, all but which of the following are methods of registering securities offerings in a state?

   A. Registration by coordination
   B. Registration by notification
   C. Registration by origination
   D. Registration by qualification

65. Monetary policy refers to actions taken by the _____ to control the money supply, often by targeting a specific rate of interest.

   A. Executive branch
   B. FDIC
   C. Federal Reserve
   D. U.S. Treasury

66. Which of the following is the formula to calculate gross national product (GNP)?

   A. GDP + Net income inflow from abroad – Net income outflow to foreign countries
   B. GDP + Net income inflow from abroad + Net income outflow to foreign countries
   C. GDP – Net income inflow from abroad – Net income outflow to foreign countries
   D. GDP – Net income inflow from abroad + Net income outflow to foreign countries

67. Which of the following typically invest in high-quality, short-term investments, such as Treasury bills, commercial paper, and negotiable CDs? The underlying investments have an average maturity of 30 to 90 days.

   A. CDs
   B. Commercial paper
   C. Money market funds
   D. Treasury bonds

68. According to FINRA Rule 2210, "correspondence" is defined as any written (including electronic) communication that is distributed or made available to _____ or fewer retail investors within any _____ calendar-day period.

   A. 25, 30
   B. 25, 60
   C. 50, 30
   D. 50, 60

69. Which of the following mutual fund share classes will charge investors a level load?

   A. Class A shares
   B. Class B shares
   C. Class C shares
   D. Class D shares

70. All but which of the following are correct regarding exchange-traded notes (ETNs)?

    A. They typically do not make interest payments to investors.
    B. They are secured debt obligations of the issuer.
    C. Their value is determined by the performance of an underlying index or benchmark on the ETN's maturity date, minus any specified fees.
    D. They trade on exchanges throughout the day, similar to stocks and ETFs.

71. Which of the following is an account that automatically transfers sums of money that exceed a certain level into a higher interest-earning option on a regular basis?

    A. Money market account
    B. Sweep account
    C. Swift account
    D. Thrift account

72. An option that can be exercised only at its expiration date is a/an _____ style option.

    A. American
    B. Asian
    C. Australian
    D. European

73. All but which of the following are correct regarding the Securities Exchange Act of 1934?

    A. It created the SEC.
    B. It regulates securities transactions in the secondary market.
    C. It is referred to as the "truth in securities" law.
    D. It includes provisions for other areas of securities law, including insider trading, antifraud, and proxy solicitation.

74. Which of the following is correct regarding defensive stocks?

    A. They are stocks that invest in the defense sector of the U.S. economy.
    B. They are stocks that are unaffected by general fluctuations in the economy.
    C. They are stocks that are tax efficient and therefore "defensive" for tax purposes.
    D. They are stocks that are unaffected by changes in interest rates.

75. Which of the following refers to an insured exchanging an existing life insurance policy for a new policy without paying tax on the investment gains earned on the original policy?

    A. 179 exchange
    B. 529 exchange
    C. 1031 exchange
    D. 1035 exchange

ANSWER KEY

1. D
A mutual fund prospectus includes fees and expenses, investment objectives, and principal risks of investing in the fund.

2. B
The potential benefit that is lost by choosing one option over another is referred to as the opportunity cost.

3. C
With certain exceptions, the Investment Advisers Act of 1940 requires that firms or sole practitioners compensated for advising others about securities investments must register with the SEC and conform to regulations designed to protect investors.

4. C
The goals of the Federal Reserve and the U.S. Treasury are full employment, stable prices, and economic growth.

5. B
An income statement is also referred to as a statement of financial performance, statement of operations, and statement of profit or loss. A statement of financial position is another name for a balance sheet.

6. C
A closed-end mutual fund has a fixed number of shares that, after original issue, trade on the secondary market. The price an investor pays when buying shares of a closed-end mutual fund is based on supply and demand.

7. D
A bond swap can potentially reduce an investor's tax liability, provide a higher rate of return, and provide investment diversification.

8. D
$8\% \times -1.5 = -12\%$
A stock with a beta of -1.5 will move 150% in the opposite direction of the market. Therefore, if the stock market increases by 8%, the stock will decrease by 12%.

9. D
The PPI (Producer Price Index) is a weighted index of prices measured at the wholesale level.

10. C
Cyclical stocks tend to prosper in growing and expanding economies, and do poorly during down business cycles.

11. B
The free credit balance refers to the cash held in an investor's margin account at a broker-dealer that can be withdrawn at any time. It may include interest, dividends, and coupon payments.

12. B

The Dow Jones Utility Average is an index comprised of 15 utility stocks, and the Dow Jones Transportation Average is an index comprised of 20 transportation stocks.

13. D

A syndicate is a group of underwriters who agree to purchase the shares of an IPO from an issuer and then sell the shares to investors.

14. A

With TIPS (treasury inflation-protected securities), investors are paid either the adjusted principal amount at maturity, or the original principal amount, whichever is greater. TIPS pay interest every six months, and their interest payments increase with inflation and decrease with deflation. They have maturities of 5, 10, or 30 years.

15. B

The preliminary prospectus is also referred to as a "red herring."

16. C

In a long call, the maximum gain is unlimited and the maximum loss is the premium paid.

17. C

The Instinet is a computerized subscriber service that serves as a vehicle for the fourth market by permitting subscribers to display bids and offers and execute trades electronically.

18. D

An indenture agreement describes the terms and conditions of a bond, including call provisions, description of collateral, and how coupon payments are determined.

19. D

According to FINRA's emergency preparedness rule, a firm must disclose to its customers how its business continuity plan addresses the possibility of a significant business disruption and how the firm plans to respond to events of varying scope. A firm's business continuity plan must be made available promptly to FINRA staff if requested, and it must be reasonably designed so the firm can meet its existing obligations to customers. The plan must be made in writing to customers when they open their account, posted on the firm's website if they maintain one, and mailed to customers upon request.

20. A

Purchasing power risk is a type of systematic risk.

21. B

Business risk is a type of unsystematic risk.

22. A

Market risk is a type of systematic risk.

23. B

Financial risk is a type of unsystematic risk.

24. A
Interest rate risk is a type of systematic risk.

25. A
Exchange rate risk is a type of systematic risk.

26. B
There is a 10% penalty on premature distributions from a qualified plan, 403(b) plan, IRA, or SEP.

27. A
The Bank Secrecy Act of 1970, also known as the Currency and Foreign Transactions Reporting Act, requires financial institutions to assist U.S. government agencies in detecting and preventing money laundering.

28 C
An investment-grade bond is one that is rated Baa3 or higher by Moody's. A high-yield bond is rated Ba1 or lower by Moody's.

29. A
Mutual fund turnover rate = Gross proceeds from sale of securities ÷ NAV

30. D
If a mutual fund charges a front-end sales load of 5% for purchases of less than $50,000, and 4% for purchases between $50,000 and $99,999, the level at which the discount becomes available is known as the breakpoint. A right of accumulation (ROA) typically provides a discount to current mutual fund purchases by combining both current and previous fund transactions to reach a breakpoint. A letter of intent (LOI) is a statement provided by an investor that expresses the intent to invest an amount over the breakpoint within a given period of time specified by the fund. In the case of ROAs and LOIs, investors are generally permitted to credit mutual fund transactions in different mutual fund classes toward breakpoint discounts.

31. D
Pegging is a manipulative trading activity that is designed to prevent the price of a security from falling.

32. D
A convertible bond is a type of corporate bond that may be converted into common stock of the issuing corporation at the bondholder's discretion. It allows an investor to share in the growth of the corporation only if the bond is converted into common stock.

33. B
The Federal Trade Commission implemented the Red Flags Rule that requires broker-dealers and other financial institutions to create a written identity theft prevention program designed to detect the warning signs of identity theft in their day-to-day operations.

34. C
Taxable equivalent yield $= 0.06 \div (1 - 0.28) = 0.0833 = 8.33\%$

35. B
A futures contract is an agreement to buy or sell a specific quantity of a commodity or financial currency at a predetermined price on a specific future date. The holder of a futures contract may purchase an offsetting contract that cancels the original position, rather than receiving delivery of the commodity. Commodities such as grains, metals, and natural gas all have tradable futures contracts.

36. A
A CUSIP is a 9-digit alphanumeric code assigned to each maturity of a municipal security issue.

37. A
ABLE accounts allow individuals with disabilities and their families to save money for disability-related expenses of the account's designated beneficiary in a tax-advantaged way.

38. C
GDP = C + I + G + (X − M)
GDP = $11.4 + $6.2 + $3.3 + ($1.8 − $2.9) = $19.8 billion

39. C
The yield to maturity (YTM) is the internal rate of return for cash flow associated with a bond, including the purchase price, coupon payments, and maturity value. It assumes that coupon payments are reinvested at the YTM rate of return for the life of the bond. When the market rate of interest for the same term and risk is higher than the coupon rate, a discount will be priced into the bond. Bonds that are riskier will have higher yields to maturity.

40. C
A normal yield curve results from short-term debt instruments having a lower yield than long-term debt instruments of the same credit quality.

41. A
The date of declaration is the date that the board of directors approves and decides that a dividend will be paid.

42. C
The date of record is the date that it is determined who owns stock in the company and is entitled to receive a dividend.

43. B
The ex-dividend date is the date that the market price of the stock adjusts for the dividend.

44. A
500 shares × $89 per share × 0.35 = $15,575

45. A
Higher coupon = Lower duration = Lower interest rate risk

46. C

The initial margin percentage is currently 50% as established by Regulation T of the Federal Reserve Board.

47. A

Qualified education costs and a first-time home purchase are among the exemptions from the 10% early withdrawal penalty from an IRA. Hardship withdrawals, and withdrawals made after separating from employment service at age 55 or older are permitted in 401(k) plans but not IRAs. Loans from IRAs are not allowed.

48. C

A TAN (tax anticipation note) is a note issued in anticipation of future tax receipts, such as receipts of ad valorem taxes that are due and payable at a set time of year.

49. B

The discount rate is the minimum interest rate set by the Federal Reserve for lending to other banks.

50. C

The Fed funds rate is the interest rate at which depository institutions (banks and credit unions) lend reserve balances to other depository institutions overnight, on a collateralized basis.

51. A

The call loan rate is the short-term interest rate charged by banks on loans extended to broker-dealers, who then use the funds to make margin loans on behalf of customers.

52. E

The prime rate is the interest rate that banks charge their most credit-worthy customers, typically large corporations.

53. D

LIBOR is the benchmark rate that international banks charge each other for short-term loans.

54. D

The substantially equal periodic payment (SEPP) exception to the 10% premature distribution penalty has no minimum age requirement.

55. B

The Patriot Act of 2001 provides the tools required to intercept and obstruct terrorism. Title III of this act is intended to facilitate the prevention, detection, and prosecution of international money laundering and the financing of terrorism.

56. A

To open a health savings account (HSA), an individual must have a high-deductible health plan (HDHP).

57. B

The maximum prison sentence for an insider trading violation is 20 years.

58. A
Buying a call and selling a put are bullish strategies. Investors choose these options when they expect the stock market to rise.

59. A
ACES (Advanced Computerized Execution System) is a subscription service operated by NASDAQ that automates trades between order entry and market maker firms that have established trading relationships with each other.

60. C
The Office of Foreign Assets Control (OFAC) administers and enforces economic and trade sanctions based on U.S. foreign policy and national security goals against targeted foreign countries and terrorist threats to the national security, foreign policy, or economy of the United States.

61. B
According to FINRA guidelines, a broker or dealer shall maintain net capital of not less than $25,000 if it acts as a broker or dealer with respect to the purchase, sale, and redemption of redeemable shares of registered investment companies.

62. D
A durable power of attorney does not survive the death of a principal or the disability of an agent.

63. B
An options disclosure document (ODD) describes the characteristics and risks of standardized options to be traded in a particular market, and is mandated by the Securities Exchange Act of 1934.

64. C
According to the Uniform Securities Act, the methods of registering securities offerings in a state are registration by coordination, registration by notification, and registration by qualification.

65. C
Monetary policy refers to actions taken by the Federal Reserve to control the money supply, often by targeting a specific rate of interest.

66. A
GNP = GDP + Net income inflow from abroad – Net income outflow to foreign countries

67. C
Money market funds typically invest in high-quality, short-term investments, such as Treasury bills, commercial paper, and negotiable CDs. The underlying investments have an average maturity of 30 to 90 days.

68. A
According to FINRA Rule 2210, "correspondence" is defined as any written (including electronic) communication that is distributed or made available to 25 or fewer retail investors within any 30 calendar-day period.

69. C

Class C mutual fund shares charge a level load.

70. B

Exchange-traded notes (ETNs) are unsecured debt obligations of the issuer and typically do not make interest payments to investors. Their value is determined by the performance of an underlying index or benchmark on the ETN's maturity date, minus any specified fees, and they trade on exchanges throughout the day, similar to stocks and ETFs.

71. B

A sweep account automatically transfers sums of money that exceed a certain level into a higher interest-earning option on a regular basis.

72. D

An option that can be exercised only at its expiration date is a European style option.

73. C

The Securities Exchange Act of 1934 created the SEC, regulates the securities transactions in the secondary market, and includes provisions for other areas of securities law, including insider trading, antifraud, and proxy solicitation. The "truth in securities" law is another name for the Securities Act of 1933.

74. B

Defensive stocks are unaffected by general fluctuations in the economy. They include food, tobacco, and oil stocks.

75. D

A 1035 exchange refers to an insured exchanging an existing life insurance policy for a new policy without paying tax on the investment gains earned on the original policy.

INDEX

Index

25451223R00098

Made in the USA
Lexington, KY
20 December 2018